THE
MYSTERIES OF
MITHRA

FRANZ CUMONT

Translated from the second revised French edition

by Thomas J. McCormack

DOVER PUBLICATIONS, INC.
NEW YORK

This Dover edition, first published in 1956, is an unabridged and unaltered republication of the second revised edition, as published by The Open Court Publishing Company in 1903.

International Standard Book Number: 0-486-20323-9
Library of Congress Catalog Card Number: 57-3150

Manufactured in the United States of America
Dover Publications, Inc.
180 Varick Street
New York, N. Y. 10014

PREFACE TO THE FRENCH EDITION

THE present work, in which we purpose to treat of the origin and history of the Mithraic religion, does not pretend to offer a picture of the downfall of paganism. We shall not attempt, even in a general way, to seek for the causes which explain the establishment of the Oriental religions in Italy; nor shall we endeavor to show how their doctrines, which were far more active as fermenting agents than the theories of the philosophers, decomposed the national beliefs on which the Roman state and the entire life of antiquity rested, and how the destruction of the edifice which they had disintegrated was ultimately accomplished by Christianity. We shall not undertake to trace here the various phases of the battle waged between idolatry and the growing Church; this vast subject, which we hope some day to approach, lies beyond the scope of the present work. We are concerned here with one epoch only of this decisive revolution, it being our purpose to show with all the distinctness in our power how and why a certain Mazdean sect failed under the Cæsars to become the dominant religion of the empire.

The civilization of the Greeks had never succeeded in establishing itself among the Persians, and the Romans were no more successful in subjecting the Parthians to their sway. The significant fact which dominates the entire history of Hither Asia is that the Iranian world and the Græco-Latin world remained forever unamenable to reciprocal assimilation, forever sundered as much by a mutual repulsion, deep and instinctive, as by their hereditary hostility.

Nevertheless, the religion of the Magi, which was the highest blossom of the genius of Iran, exercised a deep influence on Occidental culture at three different periods. In the first place, Parseeism had made a very distinct impression on Judaism in its formative stage, and several of its cardinal doctrines were disseminated by Jewish colonists throughout the entire basin of the Mediterranean, and subsequently even forced themselves on orthodox Catholicism.

The influence of Mazdaism on European thought was still more direct, when Asia Minor was conquered by the Romans. Here, from time immemorial, colonies of Magi who had migrated from Babylon lived in obscurity, and, welding together their traditional beliefs and the doctrines of the Grecian thinkers, had elaborated little by little in these barbaric regions a religion original despite its complexity. At the beginning of our era, we see this religion suddenly emerging from the darkness, and pressing forward, rapidly and simultaneously, into the valleys of the Danube and the Rhine, and even into the heart of Italy. The nations of the Occident felt vividly the superiority of the Mazdean faith over their ancient national creeds, and the populace thronged to the altars of the exotic god. But the progress of the conquering religion was checked when it came in contact with Christianity. The two adversaries discovered with amazement, but with no inkling of their origin, the similarities which united them; and they severally accused the Spirit of Deception of having endeavored to caricature the sacredness of their religious rites. The conflict between the two was inevitable,—a ferocious and implacable duel: for the stake was the dominion of the world. No one has told the tale of its changing fortunes, and our imagination alone is left to picture the forgotten dramas that agitated the souls of the multitudes when they were called upon to choose between Ormadz and the Trinity. We know the result of the battle only: Mithraism was vanquished, as without doubt it should have been. The defeat which it suffered was not due entirely to the superiority of the evangelical ethics, nor to that of the apostolic doctrine regarding the teaching of the Mysteries; it perished, not only because it was encumbered with the onerous heritage of a superannuated past, but also because its liturgy and its theology had retained too much of its Asiatic coloring to be accepted by the Latin spirit without repugnance. For a converse reason, the same battle, waged in the same epoch in Persia between these same two rivals, was without success, if not without honor, for the Christians; and in the realms of the Sassanids, Zoroastrianism never once was in serious danger of being overthrown.

The defeat of Mithraism did not, however, utterly annihilate its power. It had prepared the minds of the Occident for the reception of a new faith, which, like itself, came also from the banks of the Euphrates, and which resumed hostilities with entirely different tactics. Manichæism appeared as its successor and continuator. This was the final assault made by Persia on the Occident,—an assault more sanguinary than the preceding, but one which was ultimately destined to be repulsed by the powerful resistance offered to it by the Christian empire.

*   *   *   *   *

The foregoing rapid sketch will, I hope, give some idea of the great importance which the history of Mithraism possesses. A branch torn from the ancient Mazdean trunk, it has preserved in many respects the characteristics of the ancient worship of the Iranian tribes; and it will enable us by comparison to understand the extent, so much disputed, of the Avestan reformation. Again, if it has not inspired, it has at least contributed to give precise form to, certain doctrines of the Church, as the ideas relative to the powers of hell and to the end of the world. And thus both its rise and its decadence combine in explaining to us the formation of two great religions. In the heyday of its vigor, it exercised no less remarkable an influence on the society and government of Rome. Never, perhaps, not even in the epoch of the Mussulman invasion, was Europe in greater danger of being Asiaticized than in the third century of our era, and there was a moment in this period when Cæsarism was apparently on the point of being transformed into a Caliphate. The resemblances which the court of Diocletian bore to that of Chosroes have been frequently emphasized. It was the worship of the sun, and in particular the Mazdean theories, that disseminated the ideas upon which the deified sovereigns of the West endeavored to rear their monarchical absolutism. The rapid spread of the Persian Mysteries among all classes of the population served admirably the political ambitions of the emperors. A sudden inundation of Iranian and Semitic conceptions swept over the Occident, threatening to submerge everything that the genius of Greece and Rome had so laboriously erected, and when the flood subsided it left behind in the conscience of the people a deep sediment of Oriental beliefs, which have never been completely obliterated.

I believe I have said sufficient to show that the subject of which I am about to treat is deserving of exhaustive and profound study. Although my investigations have carried me, on many sides, much farther than I had at the outset intended to go, I still do not regret the years of labor and of travel which they have caused me. The work which I have undertaken could not have been other than difficult. On the one hand, we do not know to what precise degree the Avesta and the other sacred books of the Parsees represent the ideas of the Mazdeans of the Occident; on the other, these books constitute the sole material in our possession for interpreting the great mass of figured monuments which have gradually been collected. The inscriptions by themselves are always a sure guide, but their contents are upon the whole very meager. Our predicament is somewhat similar to that in which we should find ourselves if we were called upon to write the history of the Church of the Middle Ages with no other sources at our command than the Hebrew Bible and the sculptured *débris* of Roman and Gothic portals. For this reason, our explanations of the Mithraic imagery will frequently possess nothing more than a greater or less degree of probability. I make no pretension to having reached in all cases a rigorously exact decipherment of these hieroglyphics, and I am anxious to ascribe to my opinions nothing but the value of the arguments which support them. I hope nevertheless to have established with certainty the general signification of the sacred images which adorned the Mithraic crypts. On the details of their recondite symbolism it is difficult to throw much light. We are frequently forced to take refuge here in the *ars nesciendi.*

The following pages reproduce the "Conclusions" printed at the end of the first volume of my large work, *Textes et monuments figurés relatifs aux mystères de Mithra* (Brussels: H. Lamertin).* Stripped of the notes and references which there served to establish them, they are confined to epitomizing and co-ordinating the sum-total of the knowledge we possess concerning the origin and the characteristic features of the Mithraic religion. They will furnish, in fact, all the material necessary for readers desirous of general information on this subject. To impart the same solidity to all the various portions of the edifice we have been reconstructing has been impossible. The uncertainties and discontinuity of the tradition do not permit this. Persons desirous of examining the stability of the foundations upon which my expositions rest, should consult the critical discussions of the "Introduction" to my larger work, the purpose of which is to ascertain

---

* Large octavo, 931 pages, 507 illustrations and 9 photogravure plates. This work, which is a monument of scholarship and industry, is a complete descriptive and critical collection of all the Mithraic texts, inscriptions, references, and monuments that have been recovered from antiquity.—T. J. McC.

the meaning and value of the written documents, and especially of the figured monuments, there described.

During the long period in which this work has been in preparation I have been frequently obliged to resort to that community of interest and sentiment which unites men of science throughout the world, and I may say I have rarely appealed to it in vain. The courtesy of devoted friends, several of whom are now no more, has often anticipated the expression of my wishes, and has spontaneously placed at my disposal things which I could scarcely have dared to request. I have endeavored in my large work to make due acknowledgment to each one of them. It would not be fitting to give in this place a mere mechanical list of the names of my collaborators, and by bestowing upon them commonplace thanks to appear in the light of cancelling the indebtedness which I owe them. But it is with a feeling of profound gratitude that I recall to mind the services which have been lavished upon me, and that, having now reached the end of my task, after more than ten years, I still think of all who have aided me in completing it.

The first edition of the present work appeared in 1900, and a second was called for not long afterwards. Few changes have been made. We have added a few notes, made a few references to recent articles, and adorned the pages with a considerable number of illustrations.* The most important addition is the chapter on Mithraic sculpture, which,

---

* The illustrations of the French edition numbered twenty-two. The present English edition contains more than double that number.—T. J. McC.

in view of the extensive researches now being made as to the Oriental origins of Roman art, cannot fail to be of interest.

We have also to thank the many critics who have so kindly reviewed our *Mysteries of Mithra*, and have generously acknowledged that our reconstruction of this vanished creed rests upon an objective and complete interpretation of the sources. In a matter which is still so obscure, it was inevitable that certain divergences of opinion should have come to light, and our conclusions, at times bold, may, in certain points, have appeared to some erroneous. We have had regard for these expressions of doubt in our revision. If we have not always felt obliged to modify our opinion, it is not because we have not weighed the arguments of our critics, but because in so small a volume as the present, from which all discussions must be excluded, we had not the space to substantiate our conclusions. It is a delicate matter, we grant, to publish a text without the notes which support, explain, and modify it; but we trust that the reader will not feel too keenly this inevitable omission.

FRANZ CUMONT.

GHENT, *May 1st, 1902.*

Table *of* Contents

THE TAUROCTONOUS, OR BULL-SLAYING, MITHRA.
Bas-relief Discovered in Aquileia.

List *of* Illustrations

THE MYSTERIES OF MITHRA

THE ORIGINS OF MITHRAISM

IN THAT unknown epoch when the ancestors of the Persians were still united with those of the Hindus, they were already worshippers of Mithra. The hymns of the Vedas celebrated his name, as did those of the Avesta, and despite the differences obtaining between the two theological systems of which these books were the expression, the Vedic Mitra and the Iranian Mithra have preserved so many traits of resemblance that it is impossible to entertain any doubt concerning their common origin. Both religions saw in him a god of light, invoked together with Heaven, bearing in the one case the name of Varuna and in the other that of Ahura; in ethics he was recognized as the protector of truth, the antagonist of falsehood and error. But the sacred poetry of India has preserved of him an obscured memory only. A single fragment, and even that partially effaced, is all that has been specially dedicated to him. He appears mainly in incidental allusions,— the silent witnesses of his ancient grandeur. Still, though his physiognomy is not so distinctly

limned in the Sanskrit literature as it is in the
Zend writings, the faintness of its outlines is
not sufficient to disguise the primitive identity
of his character.

According to a recent theory, this god, with
whom the peoples of Europe were unac-
quainted, was not a member of the ancient
Aryan pantheon.   Mitra-Varuna, and the five
other Adityas celebrated by the Vedas, likewise Mithra-Ahura and the Amshaspands, who,
according to the Avestan conception surround
the Creator, are on this theory nothing but the
sun, the moon, and the planets, the worship
of which was adopted by the Indo-Iranians
"from a neighboring people, their superiors
in the knowledge of the starry firmament,"
who could be none other than the Accadian or
Semitic inhabitants of Babylonia.*   But this
hypothetical adoption, if it really took place,
must have occurred in a prehistoric epoch,
and, without attempting to dissipate the obscurity of these primitive times, it will be
sufficient for us to state that the tribes of Iran
never ceased to worship Mithra from their
first assumption of worldly power till the day
of their conversion to Islam.

In the Avesta, Mithra is the genius of the
celestial light.   He appears before sunrise on
the rocky summits of the mountains; during
the day he traverses the wide firmament in his
chariot drawn by four white horses, and when

---

* Oldenberg, *Die Religion des Veda*, 1894, p. 185.

night falls he still illumines with flickering glow the surface of the earth, "ever waking, ever watchful." He is neither sun, nor moon, nor stars, but with "his hundred ears and his hundred eyes" watches constantly the world. Mithra hears all, sees all, knows all: none can deceive him. By a natural transition he became for ethics the god of truth and integrity, the one that was invoked in solemn oaths, that pledged the fulfilment of contracts, that punished perjurers.

The light that dissipates darkness restores happiness and life on earth; the heat that accompanies it fecundates nature. Mithra is "the lord of wide pastures," the one that renders them fertile. "He giveth increase, he giveth abundance, he giveth cattle, he giveth progeny and life." He scatters the waters of the heavens and causes the plants to spring forth from the ground; on them that honor him, he bestows health of body, abundance of riches, and talented posterity. For he is the dispenser not only of material blessings but of spiritual advantages as well. His is the beneficent genius that accords peace of conscience, wisdom, and honor along with prosperity, and causes harmony to reign among all his votaries. The devas, who inhabit the places of darkness, disseminate on earth along with barrenness and suffering all manner of vice and impurity. Mithra, "wakeful and sleepless, protects the creation of Mazda" against their machinations. He combats unceasingly the spirits of evil; and the iniquitous that serve them feel also the terrible visitations of his wrath. From his celestial eyrie he spies out his enemies; armed in fullest panoply he swoops down upon them, scatters' and slaughters them. He desolates and lays waste the homes of the wicked, he annihilates the tribes and the nations that are hostile to him. On the other hand he is the puissant ally of the faithful in their warlike expeditions. The blows of their enemies "miss their mark, for Mithra, sore incensed, receives them"; and he assures victory unto them that "have had fit instruction in the Good, that honor him and offer him the sacrificial libations."*

This character of god of hosts, which has been the predominating trait of Mithra from the days of the Achæmenides, undoubtedly became accentuated in the period of confusion during which the Iranian tribes were still at war with one another; but it is after all only the development of the ancient conception of struggle between day and night. In general, the picture that the Avesta offers us of the old Aryan deity, is, as we have already said, similar to that which the Vedas have drawn in less marked outlines, and it hence follows that Mazdaism left its main primitive foundation unaltered.

Still, though the Avestan hymns furnish the

* *Zend-Avesta*, Yasht, X., *passim.*

distinctest glimpses of the true physiognomy of the ancient god of light, the Zoroastrian system, in adopting his worship, has singularly lessened his importance. As the price of his admission to the Avestan Heaven, he was compelled to submit to its laws. Theology had placed Ahura-Mazda on the pinnacle of the celestial hierarchy, and thenceforward it could recognize none as his peer. Mithra was not even made one of the six Amshaspands that aided the Supreme Deity in governing the universe. He was relegated, with the majority of the ancient divinities of nature, to the host of lesser genii or *yazatas* created by Mazda. He was associated with some of the deified abstractions which the Persians had learned to worship. As protector of warriors, he received for his companion, Verethraghna, or Victory; as the defender of the truth, he was associated with the pious Sraosha, or Obedience to divine law, with Rashnu, Justice, with Arshtât, Rectitude. As the tutelar genius of prosperity, he is invoked with Ashi-Vañuhi, Riches, and with Pârendî, Abundance. In company with Sraosha and Rashnu, he protects the soul of the just against the demons that seek to drag it down to Hell, and under their guardianship it soars aloft to Paradise. This Iranian belief gave birth to the doctrine of redemption by Mithra, which we find developed in the Occident.

At the same time, his cult was subjected to

a rigorous ceremonial, conforming to the Mazdean liturgy. Sacrificial offerings were made to him of "small cattle and large, and of flying birds." These immolations were preceded or accompanied with the usual libations of the juice of Haoma, and with the recitation of ritual prayers,—the bundle of sacred twigs (*baresman*) always in the hand. But before daring to approach the altar, the votary was obliged to purify himself by repeated ablutions and flagellations. These rigorous prescriptions recall the rite of baptism and the corporeal tests imposed on the Roman neophytes before initiation.

Mithra, thus, was adopted in the theological system of Zoroastrianism; a convenient place was assigned to him in the divine hierarchy; he was associated with companions of unimpeachable orthodoxy; homage was rendered to him on the same footing with the other genii. But his puissant personality had not bent lightly to the rigorous restrictions that had been imposed upon him, and there are to be found in the sacred text vestiges of a more ancient conception, according to which he occupied in the Iranian pantheon a much more elevated position. Several times he is invoked in company with Ahura: the two gods form a pair, for the light of Heaven and Heaven itself are in their nature inseparable. Furthermore, if it is said that Ahura created Mithra as he did all things, it is likewise said that he made him just as great and worthy as himself. Mithra is indeed a *yazata*, but he is also the most potent and most glorious of the *yazatas*. "Ahura-Mazda established him to maintain and watch over all this moving world." * It is through the agency of this ever-victorious warrior that the Supreme Being destroys the demons and causes even the Spirit of Evil, Ahriman himself, to tremble.

Compare these texts with the celebrated passage in which Plutarch† expounds the dualistic doctrine of the Persians: Oromazes dwells in the domain of eternal light "as far above the sun as the sun is distant from the earth"; Ahriman reigns in the realm of darkness, and Mithra occupies an intermediary place between them. The beginning of the Bundahish‡ expounds a quite similar theory, save that in place of Mithra it is the air (*Vayu*) that is placed between Ormazd and Ahriman. The contradiction is only one of terms, for according to Iranian ideas the air is indissolubly conjoined with the light, which it is thought to support. In fine, a supreme god, enthroned in the empyrean above the stars, where a perpetual serenity exists; below him an active deity, his emissary and chief of the celestial armies in their ceaseless combat

---

*Yasht, X., 103.

†Plutarch, *De Iside et Osiride*, 46-47; *Textes et monuments*, Vol. II., p. 33.

‡West, *Pahlavi Texts*, I. (also, *Sacred Books of the East*, V.), 1880, p. 3, *et seq.*

with the Spirit of Darkness, who from the bowels of Hell sends forth his devas to the surface of the earth,—this is the religious conception, far simpler than that of Zoroastrianism, which appears to have been generally accepted among the subjects of the Achæmenides.

The conspicuous rôle that the religion of the ancient Persians accorded to Mithra is attested by a multitude of proofs. He alone, with the goddess Anâhita, is invoked in the inscriptions of Artaxerxes alongside of Ahura-Mazda. The "great kings" were certainly very closely attached to him, and looked upon him as their special protector. It is he whom they call to bear witness to the truth of their words, and whom they invoke on the eve of battle. They unquestionably regarded him as the god that brought victory to monarchs; he it was, they thought, who caused that mysterious light to descend upon them which, according to the Mazdean belief, is a guaranty of perpetual success to princes, whose authority it consecrates.

The nobility followed the example of the sovereign. The great number of theophorous, or god-bearing, names, compounded with that of Mithra, which were borne by their members from remotest antiquity, is proof of the fact that the reverence for this god was general among them.

Mithra occupied a large place in the official cult. In the calendar the seventh month was dedicated to him and also doubtless the sixteenth day of each month. At the time of his festival, the king, if we may believe Ctesias,* was permitted to indulge in copious libations in his honor and to execute the sacred dances. Certainly this festival was the occasion of solemn sacrifices and stately ceremonies. The *Mithrakana* were famed throughout all Hither Asia, and in their form *Mihragân* were destined, in modern times, to be celebrated at the commencement of winter by Mussulman Persia. The fame of Mithra extended to the borders of the Ægean Sea; he is the only Iranian god whose name was popular in ancient Greece, and this fact alone proves how deeply he was venerated by the nations of the great neighboring empire.

The religion observed by the monarch and by the entire aristocracy that aided him in governing his vast territories could not possibly remain confined to a few provinces of his empire. We know that Artaxerxes Ochus had caused statues of the goddess Anâhita to be erected in his different capitals, at Babylon, Damascus, and Sardis, as well as at Susa, Ecbatana, and Persepolis. Babylon, in particular, being the winter residence of the sovereigns, was the seat of a numerous body of official clergy, called *Magi*, who sat in authority over the indigenous priests. The

---

* *Ctesias apud Athen.*, X., 45 (*Textes et monuments*, hereafter cited as " *T. et M.*," Vol. II., p. 10).

prerogatives that the imperial protocol guaranteed to this official clergy could not render them exempt from the influence of the powerful sacerdotal caste that flourished beside them. The erudite and refined theology of the Chaldæans was thus superposed on the primitive Mazdean belief, which was rather a congeries of traditions than a well-established body of definite dogmas. The legends of the two religions were assimilated, their divinities were identified, and the Semitic worship of the stars (astrolatry), the monstrous fruit of long-continued scientific observations, became amalgamated with the nature-myths of the Iranians. Ahura-Mazda was confounded with Bel, who reigned over the heavens; Anâhita was likened to Ishtar, who presided over the planet Venus; while Mithra became the Sun, Shamash. As Mithra in Persia, so Shamash in Babylon is the god of justice; like him, he also appears in the east, on the summits of mountains, and pursues his daily course across the heavens in a resplendent chariot; like him, finally, he too gives victory to the arms of warriors, and is the protector of kings. The transformation wrought by Semitic theories in the beliefs of the Persians was of so profound a character that, centuries after, in Rome, the original home of Mithra was not infrequently placed on the banks of the Euphrates. According to Ptolemæus,* this

* Ptol., *Tetrabibl.*, II., 2.

potent solar deity was worshipped in all the countries that stretched from India to Assyria.

But Babylon was a step only in the propagation of Mazdaism. Very early the Magi had crossed Mesopotamia and penetrated to the heart of Asia Minor. Even under the first of the Achæmenides, it appears, they established themselves in multitudes in Armenia, where the indigenous religion gradually succumbed to their cult, and also in Cappadocia, where their altars still burned in great numbers in the days of the famous geographer Strabo. They swarmed, at a very remote epoch, into distant Pontus, into Galatia, into Phrygia. In Lydia even, under the reign of the Antonines, their descendants still chanted their barbaric hymns in a sanctuary attributed to Cyrus. These communities, in Cappadocia at least, were destined to survive the triumph of Christianity and to be perpetuated until the fifth century of our era, faithfully transmitting from generation to generation their manners, usages, and modes of worship.

At first blush the fall of the empire of Darius would appear to have been necessarily fatal to these religious colonies, so widely scattered and henceforward to be severed from the country of their birth. But in point of fact it was precisely the contrary that happened, and the Magi found in the Diadochi, the successors of Alexander the Great, no less efficient protection than that which they enjoyed under the Great King and his satraps. After the dismemberment of the empire of Alexander (323 B.C.), there were established in Pontus, Cappadocia, Armenia, and Commagene, dynasties which the complaisant genealogists of the day feigned to trace back to the Achæmenian kings. Whether these royal houses were of Iranian extraction or not, their supposititious descent nevertheless imposed upon them the obligation of worshipping the gods of their fictitious ancestors. In opposition to the Greek kings of Pergamon and Antioch, they represented the ancient traditions in religion and politics. These princes and the magnates of their *entourage* took a sort of aristocratic pride in slavishly imitating the ancient masters of Asia. While not evincing outspoken hostility to other religions practised in their domains, they yet reserved especial favors for the temples of the Mazdean divinities. Oromazes (Ahura-Mazda), Omanos (Vohumano), Artagnes (Verethraghna), Anaïtis (Anâhita), and still others received their homage. But Mithra, above all, was the object of their predilection. The monarchs of these nations cherished for him a devotion that was in some measure personal, as the frequency of the name Mithradates in all their families attests. Evidently Mithra had remained for them, as he had been for Artaxerxes and Darius, the god that granted monarchs victory,—the manifestation and enduring guaranty of their legitimate rights.

This reverence for Persian customs, inherited from legendary ancestors, this idea that piety is the bulwark of the throne and the sole condition of success, is explicitly affirmed in the pompous inscription* engraved on the colossal tomb that Antiochus I., Epiphanes, of Commagene (69-34 B.C.), erected on a spur of the mountain-range Taurus, commanding a distant view of the valley of the Euphrates (Figure 1). But, being a descendant by his mother of the Seleucidæ of Syria, and supposedly by his father of Darius, son of Hystaspes, the king of Commagene merged the memories of his double origin, and blended together the gods and the rites of the Persians and the Greeks, just as in his own dynasty the name of Antiochus alternated with that of Mithridates.

Similarly in the neighboring countries, the Iranian princes and priests gradually succumbed to the growing power of the Grecian civilization. Under the Achæmenides, all the different nations lying between the Pontus Euxinus and Mount Taurus were suffered by the tolerance of the central authority to practise their local cults, customs, and languages. But in the great confusion caused by the collapse of the Persian empire, all political and

---

*Michel, *Recueil inscr. gr.*, No. 735. Compare *T. et M.*, Vol. II., p. 89, No. 1.

religious barriers were demolished. Heterogeneous races had suddenly come in contact with one another, and as a result Hither Asia passed through a phase of syncretism analo-

Fig. 1.

KING ANTIOCHUS AND MITHRA.

(Bas-relief of the colossal temple built by Antiochus I. of Commagene, 69-34 B.C., on the Nemrood Dagh, a spur of the Taurus Mountains. *T. et M.*, p. 188.)

gous to that which is more distinctly observable under the Roman empire. The contact of all the theologies of the Orient and all the philosophies of Greece produced the most startling combinations, and the competition

between the different creeds became exceed-
ingly brisk. Many of the Magi, from Armenia
to Phrygia and Lydia, then doubtless departed
from their traditional reserve to devote themselves to active propaganda, and like the Jews
of the same epoch they succeeded in gathering
around them numerous proselytes. Later,
when persecuted by the Christian emperors,
they were obliged to revert to their quondam
exclusiveness, and to relapse into a rigorism
that became more and more inaccessible.

It was undoubtedly during the period of
moral and religious fermentation provoked by
the Macedonian conquest that Mithraism
received approximately its definitive form. It
was already thoroughly consolidated when it
spread throughout the Roman empire. Its
dogmas and its liturgic traditions must have
been firmly established from the beginning of
its diffusion. But unfortunately we are unable
to determine precisely either the country or
the period of time in which Mazdaism assumed
the characteristics that distinguished it in Italy.
Our ignorance of the religious movements
that agitated the Orient in the Alexandrian
epoch, the almost complete absence of direct
testimony bearing on the history of the
Iranian sects during the first three centuries
before our era, are our main obstacles in
obtaining certain knowledge of the development of Parseeism. The most we can do is
to unravel the principal factors that combined

to transform the religion of the Magi of Asia Minor, and endeavor to show how in different regions varying influences variously altered its original character.

In Armenia, Mazdaism had coalesced with the national beliefs of the country and also with a Semitic element imported from Syria. Mithra remained one of the principal divinities of the syncretic theology that issued from this triple influence. As in the Occident, some saw in Mithra the genius of fire, others identified him with the sun; and fantastic legends were woven about his name. He was said to have sprung from the incestuous intercourse of Ahura-Mazda with his own mother, and again to have been the offspring of a common mortal. We shall refrain from dwelling upon these and other singular myths. Their character is radically different from the dogmas accepted by the Occidental votaries of the Persian god. That peculiar admixture of disparate doctrines which constituted the religion of the Armenians appears to have had no other relationship with Mithraism than that of a partial community of origin.

In the remaining portions of Asia Minor the changes which Mazdaism underwent were far from being as profound as in Armenia. The opposition between the indigenous cults and the religion whose Iranian origin its votaries delighted in recalling, never ceased to be felt. The pure doctrine of which the worshippers of fire were the guardians could not reconcile itself easily with the orgies celebrated in honor of the lover of Cybele. Nevertheless, during the long centuries that the emigrant Magi lived peacefully among the autochthonous tribes, certain amalgamations of the conceptions of the two races could not help being effected. In Pontus, Mithra is represented on horseback like Men, the lunar god honored throughout the entire peninsula. In other places, he is pictured in broad, slit trousers (*anaxyrides*), recalling to mind the mutilation of Attis. In Lydia, Mithra-Anâhita became Sabazius-Anaïtis. Other local divinities likewise lent themselves to identification with the powerful *yazata*. It would appear as if the priests of these uncultured countries had endeavored to make their popular gods the compeers of those whom the princes and nobility worshipped. But we have too little knowledge of the religions of these countries to determine the precise features which they respectively derived from Parseeism or imparted to it. That there was a reciprocal influence we definitely know, but its precise scope we are unable to ascertain. Still, however superficial it may have been,* it certainly

---

*M. Jean Réville (*Études de théologie et d'hist. publ. en hommage à la faculté de Montauban*, Paris 1901, p. 336) is inclined to accord a considerable share in the formation of Mithraism to the religions of Asia; but it is impossible in the present state of our knowledge to form any estimate of the extent of this influence.

Fig. 2.

IMPERIAL COINS OF TRAPEZUS (TREBIZOND),
A CITY OF PONTUS.

Representing a divinity on horseback resembling
both Men and Mithra, and showing that in Pontus the
two were identified.

a. Bronze coins.   Obverse: Bust of Alexander
Severus, clad in a paludamentum; head crowned with
laurel.   Reverse: The composite Men-Mithra in Oriental costume, wearing a Phrygian cap, and mounted on
a horse that advances toward the right.   In front,
a flaming altar.   On either side, the characteristic
Mithraic torches, respectively elevated and reversed.
At the right, a tree with branches overspreading the
horseman.   In front, a raven bending towards him.
(218 A.D.)

b. A similar coin.

c. Obverse: Alexander Severus.   Reverse: Men-
Mithra on horseback advancing towards the right.   In
the foreground, a flaming altar; in the rear, a tree
upon which a raven is perched.

d. A similar coin, having on its obverse the bust
of Gordianus III.   (*T. et M.*, p. 190.)

did prepare for the intimate union which was soon to be effected in the West between the Mysteries of Mithra and those of the Great Mother.

a   *b*   *c*   *d*

e   *f*   *g*

Fig. 3.

BACTRIAN COINS.

On the coins of the Scythian kings Kanerkes and Hooerkes, who reigned over Kabul and the Northwest of India from 87 to 129 A.D., the image of Mithra is found in company with those of other Persian, Greek, and Hindu gods. These coins have little direct connection with the Mysteries as they appeared in the Occident, but they merit our attention as being the only representations of Mithra which are found outside the boundaries of the Roman world.

a. Obverse: An image of King Kanerkes. Reverse: An image of Mithra.

b. The obverse has a bust of King Hooerkes, and the reverse an image of Mithra as a goddess.

c. Bust of Hooerkes with a lunar and a solar god (Mithra) on its reverse side.

d. Bust of Hooerkes, with Mithra alone on its reverse.

e, *f*, *g*. Similar coins. (*T. et M.*, p. 186.)

When, as the outcome of the expedition of
Alexander (334-323 B.C.), the civilization of
Greece spread throughout all Hither Asia, it
impressed itself upon Mazdaism as far east as
Bactriana. Nevertheless, Iranism, if we may
employ such a designation, never surrendered
to Hellenism. Iran proper soon recovered its
moral autonomy, as well as its political inde-
pendence; and generally speaking, the power
of resistance offered by Persian traditions to
an assimilation which was elsewhere easily
effected is one of the most salient traits of the
history of the relations of Greece with the
Orient. But the Magi of Asia Minor, being
much nearer to the great foci of Occidental
culture, were more vividly illumined by their
radiation. Without suffering themselves to be
absorbed by the religion of the conquering
strangers, they combined their cults with it.
In order to harmonize their barbaric beliefs
with the Hellenic ideas, recourse was had to
the ancient practice of identification. They
strove to demonstrate that the Mazdean
heaven was inhabited by the same denizens
as Olympus: Ahura-Mazda as Supreme Being
was confounded with Zeus; Verethraghna, the
victorious hero, with Heracles; Anâhita, to
whom the bull was consecrated, became Artemis Tauropolos, and the identification went
so far as to localize in her temples the fable of
Orestes. Mithra, already regarded in Babylon as the peer of Shamash, was naturally

Fig. 4.

TYPICAL REPRESENTATION OF MITHRA.
(Famous Borghesi bas-relief in white marble, now in
the Louvre, Paris, but originally taken from
the mithræum of the Capitol.)

Mithra is sacrificing the bull in the cave. The characteristic features of the Mithra monuments are all
represented here: the youths with the upright and the
inverted torch, the snake, the dog, the raven, Helios,
the god of the sun, and Selene, the goddess of the moon.
Owing to the Phrygian cap, the resemblance of the
face to that of Alexander, and the imitation of the *motif*
of the classical Greek group of Nike sacrificing a bull,—
all characteristics of the Diadochian epoch,—the original of all the works of this type has been attributed
to an artist of Pergamon. (*T. et M.*, p. 194.)

associated with Helios; but he was not subor-
dinated to him, and his Persian name was
never replaced in the liturgy by a translation,
as had been the case with the other divinities
worshipped in the Mysteries.

The synonomy thus speciously established

Fig. 5.

TAUROCTONOUS MITHRA.

Artistic Type.

(Bas-relief, formerly *in domo Andreæ Cinquinæ*, now
in St. Petersburg. *T. et M.*, p. 229.)

between appellations having no relationship
did not remain the exclusive diversion of the
mythologists; it was attended with the grave
consequence that the vague personifications
conceived by the Oriental imagination now

assumed the precise forms with which the Greek artists had invested the Olympian gods. Possibly they had never before been represented in the guise of the human form, or if images of them existed in imitation of the

Fig. 6.

TAUROCTONOUS MITHRA.

Artistic Type (Second Century).

(Grand group of white marble, now in the Vatican.
T. et M., p. 210)

Assyrian idols they were doubtless both grotesque and crude. In thus imparting to the Mazdean heroes all the seductiveness of the Hellenic ideal, the conception of their character was necessarily modified; and, pruned of their exotic features, they were rendered more readily acceptable to the Occidental peoples. One of the indispensable conditions for the success of this exotic religion in the Roman world was fulfilled when towards the second century before our era a sculptor of the school of Pergamon composed the pathetic

Fig. 7.

TAUROCTONOUS MITHRA.
Early Artistic Type.

(Bas-relief of white marble, Rome, now in the Museum of Fine Arts, Boston.)

group of Mithra Tauroctonos, to which universal custom thenceforward reserved the place of honor in the apse of the *spelæa*.*

But not only did art employ its powers to soften the repulsive features which these rude

---

* Compare the Chapter on "Mithraic Art."

Mysteries might possess for minds formed in
the schools of Greece; philosophy also strove
to reconcile their doctrines with its teachings,
or rather the Asiatic priests pretended to discover in their sacred traditions the theories of
the philosophic sects. None of these sects so
readily lent itself to alliance with the popular
devotion as that of the Stoa, and its influence
on the formation of Mithraism was profound.
An ancient myth sung by the Magi is quoted
by Dion Chrysostomos* on account of its allegorical resemblance to the Stoic cosmology;
and many other Persian ideas were similarly
modified by the pantheistic conceptions of the
disciples of Zeno. Thinkers accustomed themselves more and more to discovering in the
dogmas and liturgic usages of the Orientals
the obscure reflections of an ancient wisdom, and these tendencies harmonized too
much with the pretensions and the interest of
the Mazdean clergy not to be encouraged by
them with every means in their power.

But if philosophical speculation transformed
the character of the beliefs of the Magi, invest-
ing them with a scope which they did not
originally possess, its influence was nevertheless upon the whole conservative rather than
revolutionary. The very fact that it invested
legends which were ofttimes puerile with a
symbolical significance, that it furnished

* Dion Chrys., *Or.*, *XXXVI.*, §39, *et seq.* (*T. et M.*, Vol.
II., p. 60, No. 461).

rational explanations for usages which were
apparently absurd, did much towards insuring
their perpetuity. If the theological foundation of the religion was sensibly modified, its
liturgic framework remained relatively fixed,
and the changes wrought in the dogma were
in accord with the reverence due to the ritual.
The superstitious formalism of which the
minute prescriptions of the Vendidad were
the expression is certainly prior to the period
of the Sassanids. The sacrifices which the
Magi of Cappadocia offered in the time of
Strabo (*circa* 63 B.C.—21 A.D.) are reminiscent
of all the peculiarities of the Avestan liturgy.
It was the same psalmodic prayers before the
altar of fire; and the same bundle of sacred
twigs (*baresman*); the same oblations of milk,
oil, and honey; the same precautions lest the
breath of the officiating priest should contaminate the divine flame. The inscription of
Antiochus of Commagene (69-34 B.C.) in the
rules that it prescribes gives evidence of a like
scrupulous fidelity to the ancient Iranian customs. The king exults in having always
honored the gods of his ancestors according
to the tradition of the Persians and the
Greeks; he expresses the desire that the
priests established in the new temple shall
wear the sacerdotal vestments of the same
Persians, and that they shall officiate conformably to the ancient sacred custom. The
sixteenth day of each month, which is to be

specially celebrated, is not to be the birthday
of the king alone, but also the day which from
time immemorial was specially consecrated to
Mithra.   Many, many years after, another

Fig. 8.

KING ANTIOCHUS AND AHURA-MAZDA.

(Bas-relief of the temple of Antiochus I. of Commagene,
69–34 B.C., on the Nemrood Dagh, a spur of the
Taurus Mountains.   *T et M.*, p. 188.)

Commagenean, Lucian of Samosata, in a passage apparently inspired by practices he had
witnessed in his own country, could still deride
the repeated purifications, the interminable
chants, and the long Medean robes of the

sectarians of Zoroaster.* Furthermore, he taunted them with being ignorant even of Greek and with mumbling an incoherent and unintelligible gibberish.†

The conservative spirit of the Magi of Cappadocia, which bound them to the time-worn usages that had been handed down from generation to generation, abated not one jot of its power after the triumph of Christianity; and St. Basil‡ has recorded the fact of its persistence as late as the end of the fourth century. Even in Italy it is certain that the Iranian Mysteries never ceased to retain a goodly proportion of the ritual forms that Mazdaism had observed in Asia Minor time out of mind.§ The principal innovation consisted in substituting for the Persian as the liturgic language, the Greek, and later perhaps the Latin. This reform presupposes the existence of sacred books, and it is probable that subsequently to the Alexandrian epoch the prayers and canticles that had been originally transmitted orally were committed to writing, lest their memory should fade forever. But this necessary accommodation to the new environments did not prevent Mithraism from

*Luc., *Menipp.*, c. 6 (*T. et M.*, Vol. II., p. 22).

†Luc., *Deorum conc.*, c. 9, *Jup. Trag.*, c. 8, c. 13 (*T. et M., ibid.*)

‡Basil., *Epist. 238 ad Epiph.* (*T. et M.*, Vol. I., p. 10, No. 3). Compare Priscus, fr. 31 (I. 342 *Hist. min.*, Dind.).

§See the Chapter on "Liturgy, Clergy, &c."

preserving to the very end a ceremonial which was essentially Persian.

The Greek name of "Mysteries" which writers have applied to this religion should not mislead us. The adepts of Mithraism did not imitate the Hellenic cults in the organization of their secret societies, the esoteric doctrine of which was made known only after a succession of graduated initiations. In Persia itself the Magi constituted an exclusive caste, which appears to have been subdivided into several subordinate classes. And those of them who took up their abode in the midst of foreign nations different in language and manners were still more jealous in concealing their hereditary faith from the profane. The knowledge of their arcana gave them a lofty consciousness of their moral superiority and insured their prestige over the ignorant populations that surrounded them. It is probable that the Mazdean priesthood in Asia Minor as in Persia was primitively the hereditary attribute of a tribe, in which it was handed down from father to son; that afterwards its incumbents consented, after appropriate ceremonies of initiation, to communicate its secret dogmas to strangers, and that these proselytes were then gradually admitted to all the different ceremonies of the cult. The Iranian diaspora is comparable in this respect, as in many others, with that of the Jews. Usage soon distinguished between the different classes of neophytes, ultimately culminating in the establishment of a fixed hierarchy. But the complete revelation of the sacred beliefs and practices was always reserved for the privileged few; and this mystic knowledge appeared to increase in excellence in proportion as it became more occult.

All the original rites that characterized the Mithraic cult of the Romans unquestionably go back to Asiatic origins: the animal disguises used in certain ceremonies are a survival of a very widely-diffused prehistoric custom which still survives in our day; the practice of consecrating mountain caves to the god is undoubtedly a heritage of the time when temples were not yet constructed; the cruel tests imposed on the initiated recall the bloody mutilations that the servitors of Mâ and of Cybele perpetrated. Similarly, the legends of which Mithra is the hero cannot have been invented save in a pastoral epoch. These antique traditions of a primitive and crude civilization subsist in the Mysteries by the side of a subtle theology and a lofty system of ethics.

An analysis of the constituent elements of Mithraism, like a cross-section of a geological formation, shows the stratifications of this composite mass in their regular order of deposition. The basal layer of this religion, its lower and primordial stratum, is the faith of ancient Iran, from which it took its origin.

Above this Mazdean substratum was deposited in Babylon a thick sediment of Semitic doctrines, and afterwards the local beliefs of Asia Minor added to it their alluvial deposits. Finally, a luxuriant vegetation of Hellenic ideas burst forth from this fertile soil and partly concealed from view its true original nature.

This composite religion, in which so many heterogeneous elements were welded together, is the adequate expression of the complex civilization that flourished in the Alexandrian epoch in Armenia, Cappadocia, and Pontus. If Mithridates Eupator had realized his ambitious dreams, this Hellenized Parseeism would doubtless have become the state-religion of a vast Asiatic empire. But the course of its destinies was changed by the vanquishment of this great adversary of Rome (66 B.C.). The *débris* of the Pontic armies and fleets, the fugitives driven out by the war and flocking in from all parts of the Orient, disseminated the Iranian Mysteries among that nation of pirates that rose to power under the protecting shelter of the mountains of Cilicia. Mithra became firmly established in this country, in which Tarsus continued to worship him until the downfall of the empire (Figure 9). Supported by its bellicose religion, this republic of adventurers dared to dispute the supremacy of the seas with the Roman colossus. Doubtless they considered themselves the chosen

nation, destined to carry to victory the religion
of the invincible god. Strong in the consciousness of his protection, these audacious mariners
boldly pillaged the most venerated sanctu-

Fig. 9.

MITHRAIC MEDALLION OF BRONZE FROM TARSUS,
CILICIA.

Obverse: Bust of Gordianus III., clad in a paludamentum and wearing a rayed crown. Reverse:
Mithra, wearing a rayed crown and clad in a floating
chlamys, a tunic covered by a breast-plate, and anaxyrides (trousers), seizes with his left hand the nostrils of
the bull, which he has forced to its knees, while in his
right hand he holds aloft a knife with which he is
about to slay the animal. (*T. et M.*, p. 190.)

aries of Greece and Italy, and the Latin
world rang for the first time with the name of
the barbaric divinity that was soon to impose
upon it his adoration.

THE DISSEMINATION OF MITHRAISM IN THE ROMAN EMPIRE

IT MAY be said, in a general way, that Mithra remained forever excluded from the Hellenic world. The ancient authors of Greece speak of him only as a foreign god worshipped by the kings of Persia. Even during the Alexandrian epoch he had not descended from the plateau of Asia Minor to the shores of Ionia. In all the countries washed by the Ægean Sea, only a single late inscription in the Piræus recalls his existence, and we seek in vain for his name among the numerous exotic divinities worshipped at Delos in the second century before our era. Under the empire, it is true, mithræums are found in divers ports of the coast of Phœnicia and Egypt, near Aradus, Sidon, and Alexandria; but these isolated monuments only throw into stronger relief the absence of every vestige of the Mithraic Mysteries in the interior of the country. The recent discovery of a temple of Mithra at Memphis would appear to be an exception that confirms the rule, for the Mazdean deity was probably not introduced into that ancient city until the time of the Romans. He has not been mentioned hitherto in any inscription of Egypt or Assyria, and there is likewise nothing to show that altars were erected to him even in the capital of the Seleucidæ. In these semi-Oriental empires the powerful organization of the indigenous clergy and the ardent devotion of the people for their national idols appear to have arrested the progress of the invader and to have paralyzed his influence.

One characteristic detail shows that the Iranian *yazata* never made many converts in the Hellenic or Hellenized countries. Greek onomatology, which furnishes a considerable series of theophorous or god-bearing names indicating the popularity which the Phrygian and Egyptian divinities enjoyed, has no *Mithrion*, *Mithrocles*, *Mithrodorus*, or *Mithrophilus*, to show as the counterparts of its Menophili, its Metrodoti, its Isidori, and its Serapions. All the derivatives of Mithra are of barbaric formation. Although the Thracian Bendis, the Asian Cybele, the Serapis of the Alexandrians, and even the Syrian Baals, were successively received with favor in the cities of Greece, that country never extended the hand of hospitality to the tutelar deity of its ancient enemies.

His distance from the great centers of ancient civilization explains the belated arrival of Mithra in the Occident. Official worship was rendered at Rome to the *Magna Mater* of Pessinus as early as 204 B. C.; Isis and Serapis made their appearance there in the first century before our era, and long before this they had counted their worshippers in Italy by multitudes. The Carthaginian Astarte

had a temple in the capital from the end of
the Punic Wars; the Bellona of Cappadocia
from the period of Sulla; the *Dea Syria* of
Hierapolis from the beginning of the empire,
when the Persian Mysteries were still totally
unknown there. And yet these deities were
those of a nation or a city only, while the
domain of Mithra extended from the Indus
to the Pontus Euxinus.

But this domain, even in the epoch of
Augustus, was still situated almost entirely
beyond the frontiers of the empire; and the
central plateau of Asia Minor, which had
long resisted the Hellenic civilization, remained
even more hostile to the culture of Rome.
This region of steppes, forests, and pastures,
intersected by precipitous declivities, and
having a climate more rigorous than that of
Germany, had no attractions for foreigners,
and the indigenous dynasties which, despite
the state of vassalage to which they had been
reduced, still held their ground under the
early Cæsars, encouraged the isolation that
had been their distinction for ages. Cilicia,
it is true, had been organized as a Roman
province in the year 102 B.C., but a few points
only on the coast had been occupied at that
period, and the conquest of the country was
not completed until two centuries later. Cappadocia was not incorporated until the reign
of Tiberius, the western part of Pontus until
the reign of Nero, and Commagene and Les-

ser Armenia not definitively until the reign
of Vespasian. Not until then were regular
and immediate relations established between
these remote countries and the Occident. The
exigencies of administration and the organization of defence, the mutations of governors
and officers, the relieving of procurators and
revenue officers, the levies of troops of infantry
and cavalry, and finally the permanent establishment of three legions along the frontier of
the Euphrates, provoked a perpetual interchange of men, products, and ideas between
these mountainous districts hitherto closed to
the world, and the European provinces. Then
came the great expeditions of Trajan, of
Lucius Verus, of Septimius Severus, the sub-
jection of Mesopotamia, and the foundation of
numerous colonies in Osrhoene and as far as
Nineveh, which formed the links of a great
chain binding Iran with the Mediterranean.
These successive annexations of the Cæsars
were the first cause of the diffusion of the
Mithraic religion in the Latin world. It began to spread there under the Flavians
and developed under the Antonines and the
Severi, just as did another cult practised
alongside of it in Commagene, namely that
of Jupiter Dolichenus,* which made at the
same time the tour of the Roman empire.

According to Plutarch,† Mithra was intro-

---

*Named from the city of Doliche, now Doluk, in Commagene.
†Plutarch, *Vit. Pomp.*, 24 (*T. et M.*, Vol. II., p. 35 d.).

duced much earlier into Italy. The Romans, by this account, are said to have been initiated into his Mysteries by the Cilician pirates conquered by Pompey. Plutarch's testimony has nothing improbable in it. We know that the first Jewish community established *trans Tiberim* (across the Tiber) was composed of captives that the same Pompey had brought back from the capture of Jerusalem (63 B.C.). Owing to this particular event, it is possible that towards the end of the republic the Persian god actually had found a few faithful devotees in the mixed populace of the capital. But mingled with the multitudes of fellow worshippers that practised foreign rites, his little group of votaries did not attract attention. The *yazata* was the object of the same distrust as the Asiatics that worshipped him. The influence of this small band of sectaries on the great mass of the Roman population was virtually as infinitesimal as is to-day the influence of Buddhistic societies on modern Europe.

It was not until the end of the first century that the name of Mithra began to be generally bruited abroad in Rome. When Statius wrote the first canto of the *Thebaid*, about eighty years after Christ, he had already seen typical representations of the tauroctonous hero,* and it appears from the testimony of Plutarch that in his time (46–125 A.D.) the

---

*Statius, *Theb.*, I., 717: *Persei sub rupibus antri Indignata sequi torquentem cornua Mithram.*

Mazdean sect already enjoyed a certain noto-
riety in the Occident.* This conclusion is
confirmed by epigraphic documents. The
most ancient inscription to Mithra which we
possess is a bilingual inscription of a freedman of the Flavians (69–96 A.D.). Not long
after, a marble group is consecrated to him
by a slave of T. Claudius Livianus who was
pretorian prefect under Trajan (102 A.D.)
(Figure 10). The invincible god must also have
penetrated about the same time into central
Italy, at Nersæ, in the country of the Æqui; a
text of the year 172 A.D. has been discovered
which speaks of a mithræum that had "crum-
bled to pieces from old age." The appearance of the invader in the northern part of
the empire is almost simultaneous. It is
undoubted that the fifteenth legion brought
the Mysteries to Carnuntum on the Danube
about the beginning of the reign of Vespasian,
and we also know that about 148 A.D. they
were practised by the troops in Germany.
Under the Antonines, especially from the
beginning of the reign of Commodus, the
proofs of their presence abound in all countries. At the end of the second century, the
Mysteries were celebrated at Ostia in at least
four temples.

We cannot think of enumerating all the
cities in which our Asiatic cult was established, nor of stating in each case the reasons

*Plut., *l. c.*

why it was introduced. Despite their frequency, the epigraphic texts and sculptured monuments throw but very imperfect light on

Fig. 10.

TAUROCTONOUS MITHRA.

(Marble group of the second century, British Museum.)

The remarkable feature of this group is that not blood, but three spikes of wheat, issue from the wound of the bull. According to the Mithraic theory, wheat and the vine sprang from the spinal cord and the blood of the sacrificed animal (see the Chapter on "The Doctrine of the Mithraic Mysteries"). *T. et M.*, p. 228.

the local history of Mithraism. It is impossible for us to follow the detailed steps in its advancement, to distinguish the concurrent influences exercised by the different churches,

to draw up a picture of the work of conversion, pursuing its course from city to city and
province to province. All that we can do is
to indicate in large outlines in what countries
the new faith was propagated and who were
in general the champions that advocated it.

The principal agent of its diffusion was
undoubtedly the army. The Mithraic religion
is predominantly a religion of soldiers, and it
was not without good reason that the name
of *milites* was given to a certain grade of
initiates. The influence of the army may
appear less capable of affording an explanation when one reflects that under the emperors the legions were quartered in stationary
encampments, and from the time of Hadrian
at least (117–138 A.D.) they were severally
recruited from the provinces in which they
were stationed. But this general rule was
subject to numerous exceptions. Thus, for
example, the Asiatics contributed for a long
time the bulk of the effective troops in Dalmatia and Mœsia, and for a certain period in
Africa also. Furthermore, the soldier who
after several years of service in his native
country had been promoted to the rank of
centurion was as a rule transferred to some
foreign station; and after he had passed
through the different stages of his second
charge he was often assigned to a new garrison, so that the entire body of centurions of
any one legion constituted "a sort of micro-

cosm of the empire."* These officers were a potent source of influence, for their very position insured to them a considerable moral influence over the conscripts whom it was their vocation to instruct. In addition to this individual propaganda, which is almost totally withdrawn from our ken, the temporary or permanent transfers of single detachments, and sometimes of entire regiments, to remotely situated fortresses or camps brought together people of all races and beliefs. Finally, there were to be found side by side with the legionaries who were Roman citizens, an equal, if not a greater, number of foreign *auxilia*, who did not, like their comrades, enjoy the privilege of serving in their native country. Indeed, in order to forestall local uprisings, it was a set part of the imperial policy to remove these foreign troops as far as possible from the country of their origin. Thus, under the Flavians, the indigenous *alæ* or cohorts formed but a minimal fraction of the auxiliaries that guarded the frontiers of the Rhine and the Danube.

Among the recruits summoned from abroad to take the place of the national troops sent to distant parts were numerous Asiatics, and perhaps no country of the Orient furnished, relatively to the extent of its territory, a greater number of Roman soldiers than Commagene, where Mithraism had struck deepest

*Jung, *Fasten der Provinz Dacien*, 1894, p. xiv.

root. In addition to horsemen and legionaries, there were levied in this country, probably at the time of its union with the empire,
at least six cohorts of allies (*auxilia*). Numerous also were the native soldiers of Cappadocia, Pontus, and Cilicia, not to speak of
Syrians of all classes; and the Cæsars did not
scruple even to enroll those agile squadrons
of Parthian cavalry with whose warlike qualities they had, to their own cost, but too often
been made acquainted.

The Roman soldier was, as a rule, pious and
even superstitious. The many perils to which
he was exposed caused him to seek unremit-
tingly the protection of Heaven, and an incalculable number of dedicatory inscriptions
bears witness both to the vivacity of his faith
and to the variety of his beliefs. The Orientals especially, transported for twenty years
and more into countries which were totally
strange to them, piously preserved the memories of their national divinities, and when-
ever the opportunity offered, they did not fail
to assemble for the purpose of rendering them
devotion. They had experienced the need of
conciliating the great lord (*Baal*), whose
anger as little children they had learned to
fear. Their worship also offered an occasion
for reunion, and for recalling to memory under
the gloomy climates of the North their distant
country. But their brotherhoods were not
exclusive; they gladly admitted to their rites

those of their companions in arms, of whatever origin, whose aspirations the official religion of the army failed to satisfy, and who
hoped to obtain from the foreign god more
efficacious succor in their combats, or, in case
of death, a happier lot in the life to come.
Afterwards, these neophytes, transferred to
other garrisons according to the exigencies
of the service or the necessities of war, from
converts became converters, and formed about
them a new nucleus of proselytes. In this
manner, the Mysteries of Mithra, first brought
to Europe by semi-barbarian recruits from
Cappadocia or Commagene, were rapidly disseminated to the utmost confines of the ancient world.

From the banks of the Black Sea to the
mountains of Scotland and to the borders of
the great Sahara Desert, along the entire
length of the Roman frontier, Mithraic monuments abound. Lower Mœsia, which was
not explored until very recently, has already
furnished a number of them,—a circumstance
which will not excite our astonishment when
it is remembered that Oriental contingents
supplied in this province the deficiency of
native conscripts. To say nothing of the
port of Tomi, legionaries practised the Persian cult at Troësmis, at Durostorum, and at
Œscus, as well as at the *Tropæum Traiani*,
which the discovery of the monuments of
Adam-Klissi has recently rendered celebrated.

In the interior of the country, this cult penetrated to Montana and to Nicopolis; and it is
doubtless from these northern cities that it
crossed the Balkans and spread into the northern parts of Thrace, notably above Serdica
(Sofia) and as far as the environs of Philippop-
olis in the valley of the Hebrus. Ascending
the Danube, it gained a footing at Vimina-
cium, the capital of Upper Mœsia; but we are
ignorant of the extent to which it spread in
this country, which is still imperfectly explored.
The naval flotilla that patrolled the waters of
this mighty river was manned and even commanded by foreigners, and the fleet undoubtedly disseminated the Asiatic religion in all the
ports it touched.

We are better informed regarding the circumstances of the introduction of Mithraism into Dacia. When in 107 A.D. Trajan
annexed this barbarous kingdom to the Roman empire, the country, exhausted by six
years of obstinate warfare, was little more
than a desert. To repopulate it, the emperor
transported to it, as Eutropius* tells us, multitudes of colonists "*ex toto orbe Romano*," from
all the territories of Rome. The population
of this country was even more mixed in the
second century than it is to-day, where all the
races of Europe are still bickering and battling
with one another. Besides the remnants of
the ancient Dacians, were found here Illyrians

*Eutropius, VIII, 6.

and Pannonians, Galatians, Carians, and Asiatics, people from Edessa and Palmyra, and still others besides, all of whom continued to practise the religions of their native countries. But none of these cults prospered more than the Mysteries of Mithra, and one is astounded at the prodigious development that this religion took during the 150 years that the Roman domination lasted in this region. It flourished not only in the capital of the province, Sarmizegetusa, and in the cities that sprang up near the Roman camps, like Potaïssa and notably Apulum, but along the entire extent of the territory occupied by the Romans. Whereas one cannot find in Dacia, so far as I know, the slightest vestige of a Christian community, from the fortress Szamos Ujvar to the northern frontier and as far as Romula in Wallachia, multitudes of inscriptions, of sculptures, and of altars which have escaped the destruction of mithræums have been found. These *débris* especially abound in the central portions of the country, along the great causeway that followed the course of the valley of the Maros, the principal artery by which the civilization of Rome spread into the mountains of the surrounding country. The single colony of Apulum counted certainly four temples of the Persian deity, and the *spelæum* of Sarmizegetusa, recently excavated, still contains the fragments of a round fifty of bas-reliefs and other

votive tablets which the piety of the faithful
had there consecrated to their god.

Likewise in Pannonia, the Iranian religion
implanted itself in the fortified cities that
formed the chain of Roman defences along
the Danube, in Cusum, Intercisa, Aquincum,
Brigetio, Carnuntum, Vindobona, and even in
the hamlets of the interior. It was especially
powerful in the two principal places of this
double province, in Aquincum and in Carnuntum; and in both of these cities the causes
of its greatness are easily discovered. The
first-named city, where in the third century
the Mysteries were celebrated in at least five
temples scattered over its entire area, was
the headquarters of the *legio II adjutrix*,*
which had been formed in the year 70 A.D.
by Vespasian from sailors of the fleet stationed at Ravenna. Among the freedmen
thus admitted into the regular army, the proportion of Asiatics was considerable, and it is
probable that from the very beginning Mithraism counted a number of adepts in this irreg-
ular legion. When towards the year 120 A.D.
it was established by Hadrian in Lower Pannonia, it undoubtedly brought with it to this
place the Oriental cult to which it appears to
have remained loyal to the day of its dissolu-
tion. The *legio I adjutrix*, which had a similar

---

*One of the legions raised by the proconsuls in the Roman
provinces for the purpose of strengthening the veteran army.
—*Trans.*

origin, probably sowed the fertile seeds of
Mithraism in like manner in Brigetio, when
under Trajan its camp was transferred to that
place.

We can determine with even greater pre-
cision the manner in which the Persian god
arrived at Carnuntum. In 71 or 72 A.D., Vespasian caused this important strategic position to be occupied by the *legio XV Apol-
linaris*, which for the preceding eight or nine
years had been warring in the Orient. Sent
in 63 A.D. to the Euphrates to reinforce
the army which Corbulo was leading against
the Parthians, it had taken part during the
years 67 to 70 A.D. in suppressing the uprisings of the Jews, and had subsequently accompanied Titus to Alexandria. The losses which
this veteran legion had suffered in these sanguinary campaigns were doubtless made good
with recruits levied in Asia. These conscripts
were for the most part probably natives of
Cappadocia, and it was they that, after their
transportation to the Danube with the old
rank and file of the legion, there first offered
sacrifices to the Iranian god whose name had
been hitherto unknown in the region north
of the Alps. There has been found at Carnuntum a votive Mithraic inscription due to
a soldier of the Apollinarian legion bearing
the characteristic name of *Barbarus*. The
first worshippers of the *Sol Invictus* consecrated to him on the banks of the river a

semicircular grotto, which had to be restored
from its ruins in the third century by a
Roman knight, and whose high antiquity is
evidenced in all its details. When, some
forty years after its arrival in the Occident,
Trajan again transported the fifteenth legion
to the Euphrates, the Persian cult had
already struck deep roots in the capital of
Upper Pannonia. Not only the fourteenth
legion, *gemina Martia*, which replaced that
which had returned to Asia, but also the
sixteenth and the thirteenth *geminæ*, certain
detachments of which were, as it appears,
connected with the first-mentioned legion,
succumbed to the allurements of the Mysteries and counted initiates in their own ranks.
Soon the first temple was no longer adequate,
and a second was built, which—and this is an
important fact — immediately adjoined the
temple of Jupiter Dolichenus of Commagene.
A municipality having developed alongside
the camp and the conversions continuing to
multiply, a third mithræum was erected, probably towards the beginning of the second century, and its dimensions surpass those of all
similar structures hitherto discovered. It was
enlarged by Diocletian and the princes associated with him in 307 A.D., when they held
their conference at Carnuntum. Thus these
princes sought to give public testimony of their
devotion to Mithra in this holy city, which of
all those in the North probably contained the

most ancient sanctuaries of the Mazdean sect.

This warlike post, the most important in the entire region, seems also to have been the religious center from which the foreign cult radiated into the smaller towns of the surrounding country. Stix-Neusiedl, where it was certainly practised from the middle of the second century, was only a dependent village of this powerful city. But farther to the south the temple of Scarbantia was enriched by a *decurio coloniæ Carnunti*. Towards the east the territory of Æquinoctium has furnished a votive inscription to the *Petræ Genetrici*, and still farther off at Vindobona (Vienna) the soldiers of the tenth legion had likewise learned, doubtless from the neighboring camp, to celebrate the Mysteries. Even in Africa, traces are found of the influence which the great Pannonian city exercised on the development of Mithraism.

Several leagues from Vienna, passing across the frontier of Noricum, we come upon the hamlet of *Commagenæ*, the name of which is doubtless due to the fact that a squadron of Commageneans (an *ala Commagenorum*) was there quartered. One is not surprised, therefore, to learn that a bas-relief of the tauroctonous god has been discovered here. Nevertheless, in this province, as in Rhætia, the army does not seem to have taken, as it did in Pannonia, an active part in the propagation of the

Asiatic religion. A belated inscription of a *speculator legionis I Noricorum* is the only one in these countries that mentions a soldier; and generally the monuments of the Mysteries are very sparsely scattered in the valley of the Upper Danube, where the Roman troops were concentrated. They are not found in increased numbers until the other slope of the Alps is reached, and the epigraphy of this last-named region forbids us to assign to them a military origin.

Fig. 11.

SUN-GOD.

(Fragment from the grand bas-relief of Virunum, in Noricum. *T. et M.*, p. 336.)

On the other hand, the marvellous extension that Mithraism took in the two Germanies is undoubtedly due to the powerful army corps that defended that perpetually menaced territory. We find here an inscription dedicated by a centurion to the *Soli Invicto Mithræ* about the year 148 A.D., and it is probable that in the middle of the second century this god had already obtained a goodly number of converts in the Roman garrisons. All the regiments appear to have been seized with the contagion: the legions *VIII Augusta*, *XII Primigenia*, and *XXX Ulpia*, the cohorts and auxiliary *alæ*, as well as the picked troops of citizen volun-

Fig. 12.

MITHRAIC BAS-RELIEF OF OSTERBURKEN.

(Discovered in 1861 near the ruins of a Roman fort, in the Odenwald, Hesse. *T. et M.*, Plate VI.)

teers. So general a diffusion prevents us from telling exactly from what side the foreign religion entered this country, but it may be assumed without fear of error that, save possibly at a certain few points, it was not imported directly from the Orient, but was transmitted through the agency of the garrisons on the Danube; and if we wish to assign absolutely the circumstances of its origin we may take it for granted, with every likelihood of truth, that the eighth legion, which was transferred from Mœsia to Upper Germany in the year 70 A.D., first practised there the religion which was soon destined to become the preponderating one of this country.

Of all countries Germany is that in which the greatest number of mithræums, or places of Mithraic worship, has been discovered. Germany has given us the bas-reliefs having the greatest dimensions and furnishing the most complete representations; and certainly no god of paganism ever found in this nation as many enthusiastic devotees as Mithra. The *Agri Decumates*, a strip of land lying on the right bank of the Rhine and forming the military confines of the empire, together with the advance posts of the Roman military system between the river Main and the fortified walls of the *limes*, have been marvellously fertile in discoveries. North of Frankfort, near the village of Heddernheim, the ancient *civitas Taunensium*, three important temples have been successively exhumed (Figs. 13, 14); three others existed in Friedberg in Hesse and three more have been dug out in the surrounding country. On the other side, along the entire course of the Rhine, from Augst (Raurica) near Basel as far as Xanten (Vetera), passing through Strassburg, Mayence, Neuwied, Bonn, Cologne, and Dormagen, a series

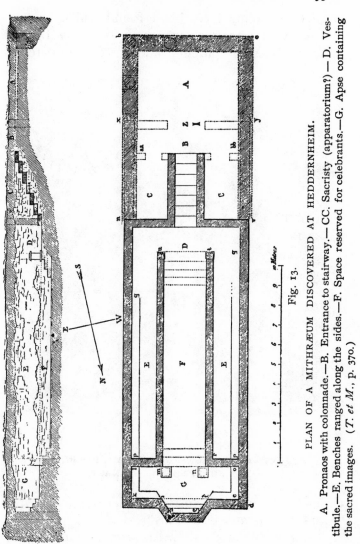

Fig. 13.

PLAN OF A MITHRÆUM DISCOVERED AT HEDDERNHEIM.

A. Pronaos with colonnade.—B. Entrance to stairway.— CC. Sacristy (apparatorium?) — D. Vestibule.—E. Benches ranged along the sides.—F. Space reserved for celebrants.—G. Apse containing the sacred images. (*T. et M.*, p. 370.)

of monuments have been found which show
clearly the manner in which the new faith
spread like an epidemic, and was disseminated

Fig. 14.

REVERSE OF THE GRAND MITHRAIC BAS-RELIEF
OF HEDDERNHEIM, GERMANY.

into the very heart of the barbarous tribes of
the Ubians and Batavians.

The influence of Mithraism among the
troops massed along the Rhenish frontier

Fig. 15.

BAS-RELIEF OF NEUENHEIM, NEAR HEIDELBERG,
GERMANY.

This monument, which escaped mutilation at the
hands of the early fanatics, was discovered in 1838 in
a cave near Neuenheim, a village on the southern
slope of the Heiligenberg, near Heidelberg, by work-
men who were laying the foundation of a farmhouse.
It is interesting as distinctly showing in a series of
small bas-reliefs twelve important scenes from the life
of Mithra, including the following: His birth from the
rocks (top of left border), his capture of the bull, which
he carries to the cave (right hand border), his ascent
to Ahura-Mazda (top border). The second scene from
the top of the left border is likewise interesting; it
represents Kronos (Zervan) handing to Zeus (Ahura-
Mazda) the scepter of the government of the world.

is also proved by the extension of this religion into the interior of Gaul.   A soldier of the
eighth legion dedicated an altar to the *Deo*

Invicto at Geneva, which lay on the military road from Germany to the Mediterranean; and other traces of the Oriental cult have been found in modern Switzerland and the French Jura. In Sarrebourg (*Pons Saravi*) at the mouth of the pass leading from the Vosges Mountains, by which Strassburg communicated and still communicates with the basins of the Mosel and the Seine, a *spelæum* has recently been exhumed that dates from the third century; another, of which the principal bas-relief, carved from the living rock, still subsists to our day, existed at Schwarzerden, between Metz and Mayence. It would be surprising that the great city of Treves, the regular residence of the Roman military commanders, has preserved only some *débris* of inscriptions and statues, did not the important rôle which this city played under the successors of Constantine explain the almost total disappearance of the monuments of paganism. Finally, in the valley of the Meuse, not far from the route that joins Cologne with Bavay (*Bagacum*), some curious remains of the Mysteries have been discovered.

From Bavay, this route leads to Boulogne (*Gesoriacum*), the naval base of the *classis Britannica* or Britannic fleet. The statues of the two dadophors, or torch-bearers, which have been found here and were certainly chiselled on the spot, were doubtless offered to the god by some foreign mariner or officer of the fleet. It was the object of this important naval station to keep in daily touch with the great island that lay opposite, and especially with London, which even at this epoch was visited by numerous merchants. The existence of a mithræum in this principal commercial and military depot of Britain should not surprise us. Generally speaking, the Iranian cult was in no country so completely restricted to fortified places as in Britain. Outside of York (*Eburacum*), where the headquarters of the troops of the province were situated, it was disseminated only in the west of the country, at Caërleon (*Isca*) and at Chester (*Deva*), where camps had been established to repel the inroads of the Gallic tribes of the Silures and the Ordovices; and finally in the northern outskirts of the country along the wall of Hadrian, which protected the territory of the empire from the incursions of the Picts and the Caledonians. All the stations of this line of ramparts appear to have had their Mithraic temple, where the commander of the place (*præfectus*) furnished an example of devotion for his subordinates. It is evident, therefore, that the Asiatic god had penetrated in the train of the army to these northern regions, but it is impossible to determine precisely the period at which he reached this place or the troops by whom he was carried there. But there is reason **for** believing that Mithra was worshipped in these countries from the middle of the second century, and that Germany* served as the intermediary agent between the far Orient

"*Et penitus toto divisos orbe Britannos.*"

At the other extremity of the Roman world the Mysteries were likewise celebrated by soldiers. They had their adepts in the third legion encamped at Lambæse and in the posts that guarded the defiles of the Aurasian Mountains or that dotted the frontiers of the Sahara Desert. Nevertheless, they do not appear to have been as popular to the south of the Mediterranean as in the countries to the north, and their propagation has assumed here a special character. Their monuments, nearly all of which date from later epochs, are due to the officers, or at least to the centurions, many of whom were of foreign origin, rather than to the simple soldiers, nearly all of whom were levied in the country which they were charged to defend. The legionaries of Numidia remained faithful to their indigenous gods, who were either Punic or Berber in origin, and only rarely adopted the beliefs of the companions with whom their vocation of arms had thrown them in contact. Apparently, therefore, the Persian religion was practised in Africa almost exclusively by those whom military service had called to these countries

---

*See *supra*, p. 1.

from abroad; and the bands of the faithful were composed for the most part, if not of Asiatics, at least of recruits drawn from the Danubian provinces.

Finally, in Spain, the country of the Occident which is poorest in Mithraic monuments, the connection of their presence with that of the garrisons is no less manifest. Throughout the entire extent of this vast peninsula, in which so many populous cities were crowded together, they are almost totally lacking, even in the largest centers of urban population. Scarcely the faintest vestige of an inscription is found in Emerita and Tarraco, the capitals of Lusitania and Tarraconensis. But in the uncivilized valleys of Asturias and Gallæcia the Iranian god had an organized cult. This fact will be immediately connected with the prolonged sojourn of a Roman legion in this country, which remained so long unsubjugated. Perhaps the conventicles of the initiated also included veterans of the Spanish cohorts who, after having served as auxiliaries on the Rhine and the Danube, returned to their native hearths converted to the Mazdean faith.

The army thus united in the same fold citizens and emigrants from all parts of the world; kept up an incessant interchange of officers and centurions and even of entire army-corps from one province to another, according to the varying needs of the day; in

fine, threw out to the remotest frontiers of
the Roman world a net of perpetual commu-
nications. Yet this was not the only way in
which the military system contributed to the
dissemination of Oriental religions. After
the expiration of their term of service, the
soldiers continued in their places of retire-
ment the practices to which they had become
accustomed under the standards of the army;
and they soon evoked in their new environment numerous imitators. Frequently they
settled in the neighborhood of their latest
station, in the little towns which had gradually replaced in the neighborhood of the
military camps the shops of the sutlers. At
times, too, they would choose their homes in
some large city of the country where they
had served, to pass there with their old comrades in arms the remainder of their days.
Lyons always sheltered within its walls a large
number of these veteran legionaries of the
German army, and the only Mithraic inscription that London has furnished us was written
by a soldier emeritus of the troops of Britain.
It was customary also for the emperor to send
discharged soldiers to some region where a
colony was to be founded; Elusa in Aquitania
was probably made acquainted with the
Asiatic cult by Rhenish veterans whom Septimius Severus (193–211 A.D.) established in
this region. Frequently, the conscripts whom
the military authorities transported to the

confines of the empire retained at heart their love for their native country, with which they never ceased to sustain relations; but when, after twenty or twenty-five years of struggle and combat, they returned to their native country, they preferred to the gods of their own city or tribe, the foreign deity whose mysterious worship some military comrade had taught them in distant lands.

Nevertheless, the propagation of Mithraism in the towns and country districts of the provinces in which no armies were stationed was due in great measure to other agencies. By her continued conquests in Asia, Rome had subjected to her domination numerous Semitic provinces. After the founding of the empire had assured peace to the entire Roman world and permanently insured the safety of commerce, these new subjects, profiting by the special aptitudes of their race, could be seen gradually concentrating in their hands the entire traffic of the Levant. As the Phœnicians and Carthaginians formerly, so now the Syrians populated with their colonies all the shores of the Mediterranean. In the Hellenic epoch they had established themselves in the commercial centers of Greece, and notably at Delos. A number of these merchants now flocked to the vicinity of Rome, settling at Pozzuoli and at Ostia. They appear to have carried on business in all the maritime cities of the Occident. They are found in Italy at Ravenna, Aquileia, and Tergeste; at Salonæ in Dalmatia, and as far distant as Malaga in Spain. Their mercantile activity even led them into the distant interior of these countries at every point where there was the least prospect of profit. In the valley of the Danube they penetrated as far as Sarmizegetusa and Apulum in Dacia, and as far as Sirmium in Pannonia. In Gaul, this Oriental population was particularly dense. They reached Bordeaux by the Gironde and ascended the Rhone as far as Lyons. After occupying the banks of this river, they flocked into the interior of the province, and Treves, the great capital of the north, attracted them in hordes. They literally filled the Roman world. Even the later invasions of the barbarians were impotent to dampen their spirit of enterprise. Under the Merovingians they still spoke their Semitic idiom at Orleans. Their emigration was only checked when the Saracens destroyed the navigation of the Mediterranean.

The Syrians were distinguished in all epochs by their ardent zeal. No people, not even the Egyptians, defended their idols with such great pertinacity against the Christians. So, when they founded a colony, their first care was to organize their national cults, and the mother country frequently allowed them generous subsidies towards the performance of this pious duty. It was in this manner that the deities of Heliopolis, of Damascus, and Palmyra first penetrated to Italy.

The word *Syrian* had in popular usage a very vague significance. This word, which was an abbreviation of *Assyrian*, was frequently confounded with it, and served to designate generally all the Semitic populations anciently subject to the kings of Nineveh, as far east as, and even beyond, the Euphrates. It embraced, therefore, the sectaries of Mithra established in the valley of this river; and as Rome extended her conquests in this quarter, the worshippers of the Persian god necessarily became more and more numerous among the "Syrians" who dwelt in the Latin cities.

Nevertheless, the majority of the merchants that founded the commercial houses of the Occident were servitors of the Semitic Baals, and those who invoked Mithra were generally Asiatics in humbler conditions of life. The first temples which this god possessed in the west of the empire were without doubt mainly frequented by slaves. The *mangones*, or slave-mongers, procured their human merchandise preferably from the provinces of the Orient. From the depths of Asia Minor they drove to Rome hordes of slaves purchased from the great landed proprietors of Cappadocia and of Pontus; and this imported population, as one ancient writer has put it, ultimately came to form distinct towns or quarters in the great capital. But the supply did not suffice for the increasing consumption of depopulated Italy. War also was a mighty purveyor of human chattels. When we remember that Titus, in a single campaign in Judæa (70 A.D.), reduced to slavery 90,000 Jews, our imagination becomes appalled at the multitudes of captives that the incessant struggles with the Parthians, and particularly the conquests of Trajan, must have thrown on the markets of the Occident.

But whether taken *en masse* after some great victory, or acquired singly by the professional traffickers in human flesh, these slaves were particularly numerous in the maritime towns, to which their transportation was cheap and easy. They introduced here, concurrently with the Syrian merchants, the Oriental cults and particularly that of Mithra. This last-named god has been found established in an entire series of ports on the Mediterranean. We signalize above all his presence at Sidon in Phœnicia and at Alexandria in Egypt. In Italy, if Pozzuoli and its environs, including Naples, have furnished relatively few monuments of the Mysteries, the reason is that this city had ceased in the second century to be the great *entrepôt* from which Rome derived its supplies from the Levant. The Tyrian colony of Pozzuoli, at one time wealthy and powerful, complains in the year 172 A.D. of being reduced to a small settlement. After the immense structures of Claudius and Tra-

jan were erected at Ostia, this latter city
inherited the prosperity of its Campanian
rival; and the result was that all the Asiatic

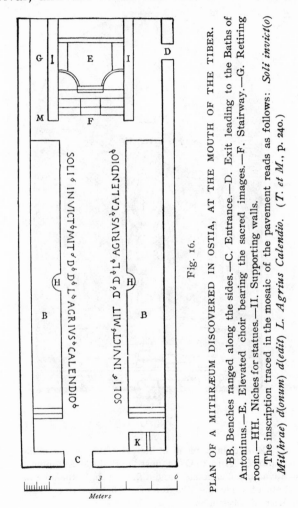

Fig. 16.

PLAN OF A MITHRÆUM DISCOVERED IN OSTIA, AT THE MOUTH OF THE TIBER.

BB. Benches ranged along the sides.—C. Entrance.—D. Exit leading to the Baths of
Antoninus.—E. Elevated choir bearing the sacred images.—F. Stairway.—G. Retiring
room.—HH. Niches for statues.—II. Supporting walls.

The inscription traced in the mosaic of the pavement reads as follows: *Soli invict(o)
Mit(hrae) d(onum) d(edit) L. Agrius Calendio*. (*T. et M.*, p. 240.)

religions soon had here their chapels and their
congregations of devotees. Yet none enjoyed

Fig. 17.

SILVANUS.

Mosaic in a niche of the vestibule of the mithræum of Fig. 16, in Ostia, near the Baths of Antoninus.
Silvanus holds in one hand a fir branch, in the other a
hatchet. See the Chapter on "The Doctrine of the
Mithraic Mysteries."

greater favor than that of the Iranian god. In the second century, at least four or five *spelæa* had been dedicated to him. One of them, constructed at the latest in 162 A.D., and communicating with the baths of Antoninus, was situated on the very spot where the foreign ships landed (Fig. 16), and another one adjoined the *metroon*, or sanctuary in which the official cult of the *Magna Mater* was celebrated. To the south the little hamlet of Antium (Porto d'Anzio) had followed the example of its powerful neighbor; while in Etruria, Rusellæ (Grosseto) and Pisæ likewise accorded a favorable reception to the Mazdean deity.

In the east of Italy, Aquileia is distinguished for the number of its Mithraic inscriptions. As Trieste to-day, so Aquileia in antiquity was the market in which the Danubian provinces exchanged their products for those of the South. Pola, at the extremity of Istria, the islands of Arba and Brattia, and the sea-ports of the coast of Dalmatia, Senia, Iader, Salonæ, Narona, Epidaurus, including Dyrrachium in Macedonia, have all preserved more or less numerous and indubitable vestiges of the influence of the invincible god, and distinctly mark the path which he followed in his journey to the commercial metropolis of the Adriatic. (See Frontispiece.)

His progress may also be followed in the western Mediterranean. In Sicily at Syracuse and Palermo, on the coast of Africa at Car-

thage, Rusicada, Icosium, Cæsarea, on the
opposite shores of Spain at Malaga and Tar-

Fig. 18.

STATUES OF TORCH-BEARERS (DADOPHORI)

From the same mithræum at Ostia, now in the
Lateran. See the Chapter on "The Doctrine of the
Mithraic Mysteries."

raco, Mithraic associations were successively formed in the motley population which the sea had carried to these cities. And farther to the north, on the Gulf of Lyons, the proud Roman colony of Narbonne doffed its exclusiveness in his favor.

In Gaul, especially, the correlation which we have discovered between the spread of the Mysteries and the extension of Oriental traffic is striking. Both were principally concentrated between the Alps and the Cévennes, or to be more precise, in the basin of the Rhone, the course of which had been the main route of its penetration. Sextantio, near Montpellier, has given us the epitaph of a *pater sacrorum*, and Aix in the Provence a presumably Mithraic representation of the sun on his *quadriga*. Then, ascending the river, we find at Arles a statue of the leontocephalous Kronos who was worshipped in the Mysteries; at Bourg-Saint-Andéol, near Montélimar, a representation of the tauroctonous god sculptured from the living rock near a spring; at Vaison, not far from Orange, a dedicatory inscription made on the occasion of an initiation; at Vienne, a *spelæum* from which, among other monuments, has been obtained the most unique bas-relief of the lion-headed god hitherto discovered. Finally, at Lyons, which is known from the history of Christianity to have had direct relations with Asia Minor, the success of the Persian religion was certainly considerable. Farther up the river, its presence has been proved at Geneva on the one hand and at Besançon and Mandeure on the Doubs, a branch of the Saone, on the other. An unbroken series of sanctuaries which were without doubt in constant communication with one another thus bound together the shores of the great inland sea and the camps of Germany.

Sallying forth from the flourishing cities of the valley of the Rhone, the foreign cult crept even into the depths of the mountains of Dauphiny, Savoy, and Bugey. Labâtie near Gap, Lucey not far from Belley, and Vieu-en-Val Romey have preserved for us inscriptions, temples, and statues dedicated by the faithful. As we have said, the Oriental merchants did not restrict their activity to establishing agencies in the maritime and river ports; the prospect of more lucrative trade attracted them to the villages of the interior, where competition was less active. The dispersion of the Asiatic slaves was even more complete. Scarcely had they disembarked from their ships, when they were scattered haphazard in every direction by the auctioneers, and we find them in all the different countries discharging the most diverse functions.

In Italy, a country of great estates and ancient municipalities, either they went to swell the armies of slaves who were tilling the vast domains of the Roman aristocracy, or they were afterwards promoted to the rank of superintendents (*actor, villicus*) and became the masters of those whose miserable lot they had formerly shared. Sometimes they were acquired by some municipality, and as public servants (*servi publici*) they carried out the orders of the magistrates or entered the bureaus of the administrations. It is difficult to realize the rapidity with which the Oriental religions were in this way able to penetrate to regions which it would appear they could never possibly have attained. A double inscription at Nersæ, in the heart of the Apennines, informs us that in the year 172 of our era a slave, the treasurer of the town, had restored a mithræum that had fallen into ruins. At Venusia, a Greek inscription 'Ηλίῳ Μίθρᾳ was dedicated by the steward of some wealthy burgher, and his name Sagaris at once proves his servile rank and Asiatic origin. The examples could be multiplied. There is not a shadow of a doubt that these obscure servitors of the foreign god were the most active agents in the propagation of the Mysteries, not only within the limits of the city of Rome itself, and in the other great cities of the country, but throughout the entire extent of Italy, from Calabria to the Alps. We find the Iranian cult practised at Grumentum, in the heart of Lucania; then, as we have already said, at Venusia in Apulia, and at Nersæ in the country of the Æqui, also at Aveia in the land of the

Vestini; then in Umbria, along the Flaminian road, at Interamna, at Spoletum, where one can visit a *spelæum* decorated with paintings, and at Sentinum, where there has been discovered a list of the patrons of a *collegium* of Mithraists; likewise, in Etruria this religion followed the Cassian way and established itself at Sutrium, at Bolsena, and perhaps at Arretium and at Florence. Its traces are no less well marked and significant to the north of the Apennines. They appear only sporadically in Emilia, where the provinces of Bologna and Modena alone have preserved some interesting *débris*, as they do also in the fertile valley of the Po. Here Milan, which rapidly grew to prosperity under the empire, appears to be the only locality in which the exotic religion enjoyed great favor and official protection. Some fragments of inscriptions exhumed at Tortona, Industria, and Novara are insufficient to prove that it attained in the remainder of the country any wide-spread diffusion.

It is certainly remarkable that we have unearthed far richer booty in the wild defiles of the Alps than in the opulent plains of upper Italy. At Introbbio, in the Val Sassina, to the east of Lake Como, in the Val Camonica, watered by the river Oglio, altars were dedicated to the invincible god. But the monuments which were consecrated to him especially abound along the river Adige (Etsch)

and its tributaries, near the grand causeway
which led in antiquity as it does to-day over
the Brenner pass and Puster-Thal to the
northern slope of the Alps into Rhætia and
Noricum. At Trent, there is a mithræum built
near a cascade; near San-Zeno, bas-reliefs
have been found in the rocky gorges; at Cas-
tello di Tuenno, fragments of votive tablets
carved on both faces have been unearthed;
on the banks of the Eisack, there has been
found a dedicatory inscription to Mithra and
to the Sun; and Mauls finally has given us the
celebrated sculptured plaque discovered in
the sixteenth century and now in the museum
at Vienna.

The progress of Mithraism in this mountainous district was not checked at the frontiers of Italy. If, pursuing our way through
the valley of the Drave, we seek for the vestiges which it left in this region, we shall
immediately discover them at Teurnia and
especially at Virunum, the largest city of
Noricum, in which in the third century two
temples at least had been opened to the initiated. A third one was erected not far from
the same place in a grotto in the midst of the
forest.

The city of Aquileia* was undoubtedly the
religious metropolis of this Roman colony,
and its important church founded many missions in the surrounding region. The cities

---

*Cf. *supra*, p. 67. See also Frontispiece.

that sprang up along the routes leading from this port across Pannonia to the military strongholds on the Danube almost without exception favorably received the foreign god: they were Æmona, the Latobici, Neviodunum, and principally Siscia, on the course of the Save; and then toward the north Adrans, Celeia, Poetovio, received him with equal favor. In this manner, his devotees who were journeying from the shores of the Adriatic to Mœsia, on the one hand, or to Carnuntum on the other, could be received at every stage of their journey by co-religionists.

In these regions, as in the countries south of the Alps, Oriental slaves acted as the missionaries of Mithra. But the conditions under which their propaganda was conducted were considerably different. These slaves were not employed in this country, as they were in the *latifundia* and the cities of Italy, as agricultural laborers, or stewards of wealthy land-owners, or municipal employees. Depopulation had not created such havoc here as in the countries of the old civilization, and people were not obliged to employ foreign hands for the cultivation of their fields or the administration of their cities. It was not individuals or municipalities, but the state itself, that was here the great importer of human beings. The procurators, the officers of the treasury, the officers of the imperial domains, or as in Noricum the governors themselves, had under

their orders a multitude of collectors of taxes,
of treasurers, and clerks of all kinds, scattered
over the territory which they administered;
and as a rule these subaltern officers were
not of free birth. Likewise, the great *entre-
preneurs* who leased the products of the mines
and quarries, or the customs returns, employed
for the execution of their projects a numerous
staff of functionaries, both hired and slave.
From people of this class, who were either
agents of the emperor or publicans whom he
appointed to represent him, are those whose
titles recur most frequently in the Mithraic inscriptions of southern Pannonia and Noricum.

In all the provinces, the lowly employees of
the imperial service played a considerable
part in the diffusion of foreign religions. Just
as these officers of the central power were
representatives of the political unity of the
empire in contrast with its regional particular-
ism, so also they were the apostles of the
universal religions as opposed to the local cults.
They formed, as it were, a second army under
the orders of their prince, and their influence
on the evolution of paganism was analogous
to that of the army proper. Like the soldiers,
they too were recruited in great numbers from
the Asiatic countries; like them, they too were
perpetually changing their residence as they
were promoted in station; and the lists of
their bureaus, like those of the legions, com-
prised individuals of all nationalities.

Thus, the imperial administration transferred from one government to another, along with its clerks and quartermasters, a knowledge of the Mithraic Mysteries. In a characteristic discovery made at Cæsarea in Cappadocia, a slave, probably of indigenous origin, an *arcarius dispensatoris Augusti* (a clerk of the imperial treasury), dedicates in very good Latin an image of the Sun to Mithra. In the interior of Dalmatia, where the monuments of the Persian god are rather sparsely scattered for the reason that this province was early stripped of its legions, employees of the treasury, the postal and the customs service, left nevertheless their names on some inscriptions. In the frontier provinces especially, the financial agents of the Cæsars must have been numerous, not only because the import duties on merchandise had to be collected here, but because the heaviest drain on the imperial treasuries was the cost of maintaining the army. It is therefore natural to find cashiers, tax-gatherers, and revenue-collectors (*dispensatores, exactores, procuratores*), and other similar titles mentioned in the Mithraic texts of Dacia and Africa.

Here, therefore, is the second way in which the Iranian god penetrated to the towns adjoining the military camps, where, as we have seen, he was worshipped by the Oriental soldiers. The general domestic service, as well as the political functions, of these administrators and officers, was the cause of the transportation of public and private slaves to all garrisons; while the constantly renewed needs of the multitudes here assembled attracted to these points merchants and traders from all parts of the world. Then again, as we have pointed out, the veterans themselves afterwards settled in the ports and the large cities, where they were thrown in contact with merchants and slaves. In affirming categorically that Mithra was introduced in this or that manner in a certain region, our generalization manifestly cannot lay claim to absolute exactitude. The concurrent causes of the spread of the Mysteries are so intermingled and intertwined, that it would be a futile task to attempt to unravel strand by strand the fibers of this entangled snarl. Having as our sole guide, as we frequently do, inscriptions of uncertain date, on which by the side of the name of the god appears simply that of an initiate or priest, it is impossible to determine in each single case the circumstances which have fostered the progress of the new religion. The more fleeting influences are almost absolutely removed from our ken. On the accession of Vespasian (69 A.D.), did the prolonged sojourn in Italy of Syrian troops, who were faithful worshippers of the Sun, have any lasting results? Did the army which Alexander Severus (222-235 A.D.) conducted into Germany, and which, as Lampridius has recorded,* was *potentissima per Armenios et Osrhœnos et Parthos* (viz., very largely composed of Armenians, Osrhœnians, and Parthians), impart a new impulse to the Mithraic propaganda on the banks of the Rhine? Did any of the high functionaries that Rome sent annually to the frontier of the Euphrates embrace the beliefs of the people over whom they ruled? Did priests from Cappadocia or Pontus ever embark for the Occident after the manner of the missionaries of the Syrian goddess, in the expectation of wresting there a livelihood from the credulity of the masses? Even under the republic Chaldæan astrologers roamed the great causeways of Italy, and in the time of Juvenal the soothsayers of Commagene and Armenia vended their oracles in Rome. These subsidiary methods of propagation, which were generally resorted to by the Oriental religions, may also have been put to profitable use by the disseminators of Mithraism; but the most active agents of its diffusion were undoubtedly the soldiers, the slaves, and the merchants. Apart from the detailed proofs already adduced, the presence of Mithraic monuments in places where war and commerce were constantly conducted, and in the countries where the vast current of Asiatic emigration was discharged, is sufficient to establish our hypothesis.

The absence of these monuments in other

*Lamprid., *Alex. Sev.*, c. 61; *cf.* Capitol., *Maximin.*, c. 11.

regions is also clear proof of our position. Why are no vestiges of the Persian Mysteries found in Asia Propria, in Bithynia, in Galatia, in the provinces adjoining those where they were practised for centuries? Because the production of these countries exceeded their consumption, because their foreign commerce was in the hands of Greek ship-owners, because they exported men instead of importing them, and because from the time of Vespasian at least no legion was charged with the defence or surveillance of their territory. Greece was protected from the invasion of foreign gods by its national pride, by its worship of its glorious past, which is the most characteristic trait of the Grecian spirit under thee mpire. But the absence of foreign soldiers and slaves also deprived it of the least occasion of lapsing from its national religion. Lastly, Mithraic monuments are almost completely missing in the central and western parts of Gaul, in the Spanish peninsula, and in the south of Britain, and they are rare even in the interior of Dalmatia. In these places also no permanent army was stationed; there was consequently no importation of Asiatics; while there was also in these countries no great center of international commerce to attract them.

On the other hand, the city of Rome is especially rich in discoveries of all kinds, more so in fact than any of the provinces. In fact Mithra found in no other part of the empire

conditions so eminently favorable to the success of his religion. Rome always had a large
garrison made up of soldiers drawn from all
parts of the empire, and the veterans of the
army, after having been honorably discharged,
flocked thither in great numbers to spend the
remainder of their days. An opulent aristocracy resided here, and their palaces, like those
of the emperor, were filled with thousands of
Oriental slaves. It was the seat of the central
imperial administration, the official slaves of
which thronged its bureaus. Finally, all whom
the spirit of adventure, or disaster, had driven
hither in search of fame and fortune flocked
to this "caravansary of the universe," and carried thither their customs and their religions.
Collaterally, the presence in Rome of numbers of Asiatic princelings, who lived there,
either as hostages or fugitives, with their families and retinues, also abetted the propagation
of the Mazdean faith.

Like the majority of the foreign gods, Mithra
undoubtedly had his first temples outside of
the *pomoerium*, or religious limits. Many of
his monuments have been discovered beyond
these boundaries, especially in the vicinity of
the prætorian camp; but before the year 181
A.D. he had overleaped the sacred barriers
and established himself in the heart of the
city. It is unfortunately impossible to follow
step by step his progress in the vast metropolis. Records of exact date and indubitable

origin are too scarce to justify us in reconstructing the local history of the Persian religion in Rome. We can only determine in a
general way the high degree of splendor
which it attained there. Its vogue is attested
by a hundred or more inscriptions, by more
than seventy-five fragments of sculpture, and
by a series of temples and chapels situated in
all parts of the city and its environs. The
most justly celebrated of these *spelæa* is the
one that still existed during the Renaissance
in a cave of the Capitol, and from which the
grand Borghesi bas-relief now in the Louvre
was taken. (See Fig. 4.) To all appearances,
this monument dates from the end of the second century.

It was at this period that Mithra emerged
from the partial obscurity in which he had
hitherto lived, to become one of the favorite
gods of the Roman aristocracy and the imperial court. We have seen him arrive from the
Orient a despised deity of the deported or
emigrant Asiatics. It is certain that he
achieved his first conquests among the lower
classes of society, and it is an important fact
that Mithraism long remained the religion of
the lowly. The most ancient inscriptions are
eloquent evidence of the truth of this asser-
tion, for they emanated without exception
from slaves or freedmen, from soldiers active
or retired. But the high destinies to which
freedmen were permitted to aspire under the

empire are well known; while the sons of veterans or of centurions not infrequently became citizens of wealth and influence. Thus, by a natural evolution the religion transplanted to Latin soil was bound to wax great in wealth as well as in influence, and soon to count among its sectaries influential functionaries at the capital, and church and town dignitaries in the municipalities. Under the Antonines (138-180 A.D.), literary men and philosophers began to grow interested in the dogmas and rites of this Oriental cult. The wit Lucian parodied their ceremonies*; and in 177 A.D. Celsus in his *True Discourse* undoubtedly pits its doctrines against those of Christianity.†
At about the same period a certain Pallas devoted to Mithraism a special work, and Porphyry cites a certain Eubulus who had published *Mithraic Researches‡* in several books. If this literature were not irrevocably lost to us, we should doubtless re-read in its pages the story of entire Roman squadrons, both officers and soldiers, passing over to the faith of the hereditary enemies of the empire, and of great lords converted by the slaves of their own establishments. The monuments frequently mention the names of slaves beside

---

*Lucian, *Menipp.*, c. 6 *et seq.* *Cf. Deor. concil.*, c. 9; *Jup. trag.*, c. 8, 13 (*T. et M.*, Vol. II, p. 22).

†Origen, *Contra. Cels.*, I. 9 (*T. et M.*, Vol. II, p. 30).

‡*Porphyr.*, *De antr. nymph.*, c. 5; *De abstin.*, II. 56, IV. 16 (*cf. T. et M.*, Vol. II, p. 39 *et seq.* and I., p. 26 *et seq.*

those of freedmen, and sometimes it is the former that have attained the highest rank among the initiates. In these societies, the last frequently became the first, and the first the last,—to all appearances at least.

One capital result emerges from the detailed facts which we have adduced. It is that the spread of the Persian Mysteries must have taken place with extreme rapidity. With the suddenness of a flash of gunpowder, they make their appearance almost simultaneously in countries far removed from one another: in Rome, at Carnuntum on the Danube, and in the *Agri Decumates.* Manifestly, this reformed church of Mazdaism exercised on the society of the second century a powerful fascination, of which to-day we can only imperfectly ascertain the causes.

But to the natural allurements which drew crowds to the feet of the tauroctonous god was added an extrinsic element of the highest efficacy: the imperial favor. Lampridius* informs us that Commodus (180-192 A.D.) was initiated into the Mysteries and took part in the bloody ceremonies of its liturgy, and the inscriptions prove that this condescension of the monarch toward the priests of Mithra created an immense stir in the Roman world, and told enormously in favor of the Persian religion. From this moment the exalted dig-

---

*Lamprid., *Commod.*, c. 9 (*T. et M.*, Vol. II, p. 21). See *infra*, Chap. III, p. 73.

nitaries of the empire are seen to follow the example of their sovereign and to become zealous cultivators of the Iranian cult. Tribunes, prefects, legates, and later *perfectissimi* and *clarissimi*, are frequently mentioned as authors of the votive inscriptions; and until the downfall of paganism the aristocracy remained attached to the solar god that had so long enjoyed the favor of princes. But to understand the political and moral motives of the kindly reception which these dignitaries accorded to the new faith, it will be necessary to expound the Mithraic doctrines concerning the sovereign power and their connection with the theocratic claims of the Cæsars.

MITHRA AND THE IMPERIAL POWER OF ROME.

OWING to the relatively late epoch of their propagation, the Mysteries of Mithra escaped the persecutions that had been the destiny of the other Oriental cults that had preceded them in Rome, especially that of Isis. Among the astrologers or "Chaldæans" who had been expelled from Italy at various times under the first emperors, there may possibly have been some that rendered homage to the Persian gods; but these wandering soothsayers, who, in spite of the pronunciamentos of the senate, which were as impotent as they were severe, invariably made their appearance again in the capital, no more preached a definite religion than they constituted a regular clergy. When, toward the end of the first century, Mithraism began to spread throughout the Occident, the haughty reserve or outspoken hostility which had anciently characterized the attitude of the Roman policy toward foreign missionaries began to give way to a spirit of benevolent tolerance, where not of undisguised favor. Nero (54-68 A.D.) had already expressed a desire to be initiated into the ceremonies of Mazdaism by the Magi whom King Tiridates of Armenia had brought

with him to Rome, and this last-mentioned
prince had worshipped in Nero an emanation
of Mithra himself.

Unfortunately, we have no direct information regarding the legal status of the associations of the *Cultores Solis invicti Mithræ*. No
text tells us whether the existence of these
brotherhoods was at first simply tolerated, or
whether, having been recognized by the State,
they acquired at the outset the right of owning
property and of transacting business. In any
event, it is quite unlikely that a religion that
had always counted so many adherents in the
administration and the army should have been
left by the sovereign for any length of time in
an anomalous condition. Perhaps, in order
to acquire legal standing, these religious societies were organized as burial associations, and
acquired thus the privileges accorded to this
species of corporations. It would appear,
however, that they had resorted to a still more
efficacious expedient. From the moment of
the discovery of traces of the Persian cult in
Italy, we find it intimately associated with that
of the *Magna Mater* (or Great Mother) of Pessinus, which had been solemnly adopted by the
Roman people three centuries before. Further, the sanguinary ceremony of the *taurobolium*, or baptism in the blood of a bull, which
had, under the influence of the old Mazdean
belief, been adopted into the liturgy of the
Phrygian goddess, was encouraged, probably

from the period of Marcus Aurelius (161-180 A.D.), by grants of civil immunities.* True, we are still in doubt whether this association of the two deities was officially confirmed by the senate or the prince. Had this been done, the foreign god would at once have acquired the rights of Italian citizenship and would have been accorded the same privileges with Cybele or the Bellona of Comana. But even lacking all formal declaration on the part of the public powers, there is every reason to believe that Mithra, like Attis, whom he had been made to resemble, was linked in worship with the Great Mother and participated to the full in the official protection which the latter enjoyed. Yet the clergy appear never to have received a regular donation from the treasury, although the imperial *fiscus* and the municipal coffers were in exceptional cases opened for their benefit.

Toward the end of the second century, the more or less circumspect complaisance with which the Cæsars had looked upon the Iranian Mysteries was suddenly transformed into effective support. Commodus (180-192 A.D.) was admitted among their adepts and participated in their secret ceremonies, and the discovery of numerous votive inscriptions, either for the welfare of this prince or bearing the date of his reign, gives us some inkling of the impetus which this imperial conversion imparted to the

---

*See the Chapter "Mithra and the Religions of the Empire."

Mithraic propaganda. After the last of the
Antonine emperors had thus broken with the
ancient prejudice, the protection of his successors appears to have been definitely assured to

Fig. 19.

PEDESTAL FOUND AT CARNUNTUM.

The gift of Diocletian, Valerius, and Licinius. (*T. et
M.*, p. 491.)

the new religion. From the first years of the
third century onward it had its chaplain in the
palace of the Augusti, and its votaries are seen
to offer vows and sacrifices for the protection
of Severus and Philippus. Aurelian (270-275

A.D.), who instituted the official cult of the
Sol invictus, could have had only sentiments of
sympathy with the god that was regarded as
identical with the one whom he caused his
pontiffs to worship. In the year 307 A.D.,
Diocletian, Galerius, and Licinius, at their
conference in Carnuntum, dedicated with one
accord a temple to Mithra *fautori imperii sui*
(Figure 19), and the last pagan that occupied the
throne of the Cæsars, Julian the Apostate, was
an ardent votary of this tutelar god, whom he
caused to be worshipped in Constantinople.

Such unremitting favor on the part of monarchs of so divergent types and casts of mind
cannot have been the result of a passing
vogue or of individual fancies. It must have
had deeper causes. If for two hundred years
the rulers of the empire show so great a predilection for this foreign religion, born among
the enemies whom the Romans never ceased
to combat, they were evidently constrained to
do so by some reason of state. In point of
fact, they found in its doctrines a support for
their personal policy and a staunch advocacy
of the autocratic pretensions which they were
so energetically endeavoring to establish.

We know the slow evolution which gradually
transformed the principate that Augustus had
founded into a monarchy existing by the grace
of God. The emperor, whose authority was
theoretically derived from the nation, was at
the outset simply the first magistrate of Rome.

As the heir of the tribunes and as supreme pontiff, he was, by very virtue of his office, already inviolable and invested with a sacred character; but, just as his power, which was originally limited by law, ended after a succession of usurpations in complete absolutism, so also by a parallel development the prince, the plenipotentiary of the nation, became the representative of God on earth, nay, even God himself (*dominus et deus*).   Immediately after the battle of Actium (31 B.C.), we see arising a movement which is diametrically opposed to the original democratic fiction of Cæsarism. The Asiatic cities forthwith made haste to erect temples in honor of Augustus and to render homage to him in a special cult.   The monarchical memories of these peoples had never faded.   They had no understanding for the subtle distinctions by which the Italians were endeavoring to overreach themselves. For them, a sovereign was always a king (βασιλεύς) and a god (θεός).   This transformation of the imperial power was a triumph of the Oriental genius over the Roman mind,— the triumph of the religious idea over the conception of law.

Several historians have studied in detail the organization of this worship of the emperors and have shed light on its political importance. But they have not discerned so clearly perhaps the nature of its theological foundation.   It is not sufficient to point out that at a certain epoch the princes not only received divine honors after their death, but were also made the recipients of this homage during their reign. It must be explained why this deification of a living person, how this new species of apotheosis, which was quite contrary to common sense and to sound Roman tradition, was in the end almost universally adopted. The sullen resistance of public opinion was overcome when the religions of Asia vanquished the masses of the population. These religions propagated in Italy dogmas which tended to raise the monarchs above the level of humankind, and if they won the favor of the Cæsars, and particularly of those who aspired to absolute power, it is because they supplied a dogmatic justification of their despotism. In place of the old principle of popular sovereignty was substituted a reasoned faith in supernatural influence. We shall now essay to show what part Mithraism played in this significant transformation, concerning which our historical sources only imperfectly inform us.

Certain plausible appearances have led some people to suppose that the Romans drew all ideas of this class from Egypt. Egypt, whose institutions in so many directions inspired the administrative reforms of the empire, was also in a position to furnish it with a consummate model of a theocratic government. According to the ancient beliefs of that country, not only did the royal race derive its origin from the

sun-god Râ, but the soul of each sovereign
was a double detached from the sun-god
Horus. All the Pharaohs were thus successive incarnations of the great day-star. They
were not only the representatives of divinities,
but living gods worshipped on the same footing with those that traversed the skies, and
their insignia resembled those of this divinity.

The Achæmenides, who became masters of
the valley of the Nile, and after them also the
Ptolemies, inherited the homage which had
been paid to the ancient Egyptian kings, and
it is certain that Augustus and his successors,
who scrupulously respected all the religious
usages of the country as well as its political
constitution, there suffered themselves to be
made the recipients of the same character that
a tradition of thirty centuries had accorded to
the potentates of Egypt.

From Alexandria, where even the Greeks
themselves accepted it, this theocratic doctrine
was propagated to the farthest confines of the
empire. The priests of Isis were its most popular missionaries in Italy. The proselytes
whom they had made in the highest classes of
society became imbued with it; the emperors,
whose secret or avowed ambitions this attribute flattered, soon encouraged it openly.
Yet, although their policy would have been
favored by a diffusion of the Egyptian doctrine, they were still impotent to impose its
tenets at once and unrestrictedly. From the

first century on they had suffered themselves
to be called *deus noster* by their domestic servants and their ministers, who were already
half Oriental, but they had not the audacity
at that period to introduce this name into
their official titles. Certain of the Cæsars, a
Caligula or a Nero, could dream of playing on
the stage of the world the rôle which the
Ptolemies played in their smaller kingdom.
They could persuade themselves that different gods had taken life in their own persons;
but enlightened Romans were invariably
outraged at their extravagances. The Latin
spirit rebelled against the monstrous fiction
created by the Oriental imagination. The
apotheosis of a reigning prince encountered
obstinate adversaries even in a much later
time, among the last of the pagans. For the
general acceptance of the doctrine a theory
far less crude than that of the Alexandrian
epiphany was needed. And it was the religion
of Mithra that furnished this doctrine.

The Persians, like the Egyptians, prostrated
themselves before their sovereigns, but they
nevertheless did not regard them as gods.
When they rendered homage to the "demon"
of their king, as they did at Rome to the
"genius" of Cæsar (*genius Cæsaris*), they worshipped only the divine element that resided in
every man and formed part of his soul. The
majesty of the monarchs was sacred solely
because it descended to them from Ahura-

Mazda, whose divine wish had placed them on their throne. They ruled "by the grace" of the creator of heaven and earth. The Iranians pictured this "grace" as a sort of supernatural fire, as a dazzling aureole, or nimbus of "glory," which belonged especially to the gods, but which also shed its radiance upon princes and consecrated their power. The *Hvarenô*, as the Avesta calls it, illuminated legitimate sovereigns and withdrew its light from usurpers as from impious persons, who were soon destined to lose, along with its possession, both their crowns and their lives. On the other hand, those who were deserving of obtaining and protecting it received as their reward unceasing prosperity, great fame, and perpetual victory over their enemies.

This peculiar conception of the Persians had no counterpart in the other mythologies, and the foreign nations of antiquity likened the Mazdean "Glory," not very correctly, to Fortune. The Semites identified it with their *Gadâ*, the Grecians translated the name by Τύχη, or Tyche. The different dynasties that succeeded the fall of the Achæmenides and endeavored to trace back their genealogy to some member of the ancient reigning house, naturally rendered homage to this special Tyche whose protection was at once the consequence and the demonstration of their legitimacy. We see the *Hvarenô* honored alike, and for the same motives, by the kings of

Cappadocia, Pontus, and Bactriana; and the
Seleucids, who long ruled over Iran, were also
regarded as the *protégés* of the Fortune who
had been sent by the Supreme God. In his
burial inscription, Antiochus of Commagene
appears to have gone so far as to identify himself with the goddess. The Mazdean ideas
concerning monarchical power thus spread into
Occidental Asia at the same time with Mithraism. But, like this latter, it was interwoven
with Semitic doctrines. The belief that fatality
gave and took away the crown again made its
appearance even among the Achæmenides.
Now, according to the Chaldæans, destiny is
necessarily determined by the revolution of
the starry heavens, and the brilliant celestial
body that appears to command all its comrades was considered as the royal star *par excellence*. Thus, the invincible Sun ("Ηλιος ἀνίκητος), identified with Mithra, was during the
Alexandrian period generally considered as the
dispenser of the *Hvarenô* that gives victory.
The monarch upon whom this divine grace descended was lifted above ordinary mortals and
revered by his subjects as a peer of the gods.
After the downfall of the Asiatic principalities,
the veneration of which their dynasties had
been the object was transferred to the Roman
emperors. The Orientals forthwith saluted in
the persons of these rulers the elect of God,
to whom the Fortune of kings had given
omnipotent power. According as the Syrian

religions, and especially the Mysteries of
Mithra, were propagated in Rome, the ancient
Mazdean theory, more or less tainted with
Semitism, found increasing numbers of champions in the official Roman world. We see it
making its appearance there, at first timidly
but afterward more and more boldly, in the
sacred institutions and the official titles of the
emperors, the meaning of which it alone enables us to fathom.

Since the republican epoch the "Fortune
of the Roman people" had been worshipped
under different names at Rome. This ancient
national cult soon became impregnated with
the beliefs of the Orient, where not only every
country but every city worshipped its own
divine Destiny. When Plutarch tells us that
Tyche forsook the Assyrians and the Persians,
crossed Egypt and Syria, and took her abode
on the Palatine Hill, his metaphor is true in
quite a different sense from that which he had
in mind. Also the emperors, imitating their
Asiatic predecessors, easily succeeded in causing to be worshipped by the side of this goddess of the State, that other goddess who was
the special protectress of their own person.
The *Fortuna Augusti* had appeared on the
coins since Vespasian, and as formerly the
subjects of the Diadochi, so now those of
the Cæsars, swore by the Fortune of their
princes. The superstitious devotion of these
rulers to their patron goddess was so great

that in the second century at least they constantly had before them, even during sleep or
on voyages, a golden statue of the goddess,
which on their death they transmitted to their
successor and which they invoked under the
name of *Fortuna regia*, a translation of Τύχη
βασιλέως. In fact, when this safeguard abandoned them they were doomed to destruction
or at least to reverses and calamities; as long
as it abided with them, they knew only success and prosperity.

After the reign of Commodus (180-192
A.D.), from which the triumph at Rome of the
Oriental cults and especially of the Mithraic
Mysteries dates, we see the emperors officially taking the titles of *pius*, *felix*, and *invictus*, which appellations from the third century on regularly formed part of the imperial
protocols. These epithets were inspired by
the special fatalism which Rome had borrowed from the Orient. The monarch is
pius (pious) because his devotion alone can
secure the continuance of the special favor
which Heaven has bestowed on him; he is
felix, happy, or rather fortunate (εὐτυχής), for
the definite reason that he is illuminated by
the divine *Grace;* and finally he is "invincible"
because the defeat of the enemies of the
empire is the most signal indication that his
tutelary "Grace" has not ceased to attend
him. Legitimate authority is not given by
heredity or by a vote of the senate, but by the

gods; and it is manifested in the shape of victory.

All this conforms to the ancient Mazdean ideas, and the employment of the last of the three adjectives mentioned further betrays the influence of the astrological theories which were mingled with Parseeism. *Invictus*, 'Aví-κητος, is, as we have seen, the ordinary attribute of the sidereal gods imported from the Orient, and especially so of the Sun. The emperors evidently chose this appellation to emphasize their resemblance to the celestial divinity, the idea of whom it immediately evoked. The doctrine that the fate of states, like that of individuals, was inseparably conjoined with the course of the stars, was accompanied with the corollary that the chief of the planetary bodies was arbiter of the Fortune of kings. It was he that raised them to their thrones, or deposed them; it was he that assured to them their triumphs and visited upon them their disasters. The Sun is regarded as the companion (*comes*) of the emperor and as his personal saviour (*conservator*). We have already seen that Diocletian revered in Mithra the *fautor imperii sui*, or patron of his empire.

In assuming the surname *invictus* (invincible), the Cæsars formally announced the intimate alliance which they had contracted with the Sun, and they tended more and more to emphasize their likeness to him. The same reason induced them to assume the still more ambitious epithet of "eternal," which, having long been employed in ordinary usage, was in the third century finally introduced into the official formularies. This epithet, like the first, is borne especially by the solar divinities of the Orient, the worship of whom spread in Italy at the beginning of our era. Applied to the sovereigns, it reveals more clearly than the first-named epithet the conviction that from their intimate companionship with the Sun they were united to him by an actual identity of nature.

This conviction is also manifested in the usages of the court. The celestial fire which shines eternally among the stars, always victorious over darkness, had as its emblem the inextinguishable fire that burned in the palace of the Cæsars and which was carried before them in the official ceremonies. This lamp, constantly lighted, had also served the Persian kings as an image of the perpetuity of their power; and it passed with the mystical ideas of which it was the expression to the Diadochi, and from them to the Romans.

Also, the radiate crown which, in imitation of the Seleucids and the Ptolemies, the emperors had adopted since Nero as the symbol of their sovereignty, is fresh evidence of these politico-religious tendencies. Symbolical of the splendor of the Sun and of the rays which he gave forth, it appeared to render the monarch the simulacrum of the planet-god whose brilliancy dazzles the eyes.

What was the sacred relation established between the radiant disc which illuminated the heavens and the human image which represented it on earth? The loyalist zeal of the Orientals knew no bounds in its apotheosis. The Sassanian kings, as the Pharaohs before them, proclaimed themselves "brothers of the sun and the moon"; and the Cæsars were almost similarly regarded in Asia as the successive Avatars of Helios. Certain autocrats approved of being likened to this divinity and caused statues to be erected that showed them adorned with his attributes. They suffered themselves even to be worshipped as emanations of Mithra. But these insensate pretensions were repudiated by the sober sense of the Latin peoples. As above remarked, the Occident studiously eschewed such absolute affirmations; they were content with metaphors; they were fond of comparing the sovereign who governed the inhabited world and whom nothing that occurred in it could escape, to the celestial luminary that lighted the universe and controlled its destinies. They preferred to use obscure expressions which admitted of all kinds of interpretations. They conceded that the prince was united with the immortals by some relation of kinship, but they were chary of precisely defining its character. Nevertheless, the conception that the

50446

Sun had the emperor under his protection and that supernatural effluvia descended from the one to the other, gradually led to the notion of their consubstantiality.

Now, the psychology taught in the Mysteries furnished a rational explanation of this consubstantiality and supplied it almost with a scientific foundation. According to these doctrines the souls pre-existed in the empyrean, and when they descended to earth to animate the bodies in which they were henceforward to be confined, they traversed the spheres of the planets and received from each some of its planetary qualities. For all the astrologers, the Sun, as before remarked, was the royal star, and it was consequently he that gave to his chosen ones the virtues of sovereignty and called them to kingly dominion.

It will be seen immediately how these theories favored the pretensions of the Cæsars. They were lords of the world by right of birth (*deus et dominus natus*), because they had been destined to the throne by the stars from their very advent into the world. They were divine, for there were in them some of the elements of the Sun, of which they were in a sense the passing incarnation. Descended from the starry heavens, they returned there after their death to pass eternity in the company of the gods, their equals. The common mortal pictured the emperor after his death, like Mithra at the end of his career, as borne heavenward by Helios in his resplendent chariot.

Thus, the dogmatology of the Persian Mysteries combined two theories of different origin, both of which tended to lift princes above the level of humankind. On the one side, the ancient Mazdean conception of *Hvarenô* had become the "Fortune of the King," illuminating him with celestial grace and bringing him victory. On the other hand, the idea that the soul of the monarch, at the moment when destiny caused its descent to the terrestrial spheres, received from the Sun its dominating power, gave rise to the contention that its recipient shared in the divinity of that star, and was its representative on earth.

These beliefs may appear to us to-day as absurd, or even monstrous, but they controlled nevertheless for centuries millions of men of the most different types and nationalities, and united them under the banner of the same monarchical faith. If the educated classes, who through literary tradition always preserved some remnant of the ancient republican spirit, cherished a measure of skepticism in this regard, the popular sentiment certainly accepted these theocratical chimeras, and suffered themselves to be governed by them as long as paganism lasted. It may even be said that these conceptions survived the breaking of the idols, and that the veneration of the masses as well as the ceremonial of the court

never ceased to consider the person of the
sovereign as endued with essence superhuman.
Aurelian (270-275 A.D.) had essayed to establish an official religion broad enough to embrace all the cults of his dominions and which
would have served, as it had among the Persians, both as the justification and the prop of
imperial absolutism. His hopes, however,
were blasted, mostly by the recalcitrance of
the Christians. But the alliance of the throne
with the altar, of which the Cæsars of the
third century had dreamed, was realized under
another form; and by a strange mutation of fortune the Church itself was called upon to support the edifice whose foundations it had shattered. The work for which the priests of
Serapis, of Baal, and of Mithra had paved the
way was achieved without them and in opposition to them. Nevertheless, they had been
the first to preach in Occidental parts the doctrine of the divine right of kings, and had thus
become the initiators of a movement of which
the echoes were destined to resound even "to
the last syllable of recorded time."

THE DOCTRINE OF THE MITHRAIC
MYSTERIES

FOR more than three centuries Mithraism was practised in the remotest provinces of the Roman empire and under the most diverse conditions. It is not to be supposed for a moment that during this long period its sacred traditions remained unchanged, or that the philosophies which one after another swayed the minds of antiquity, or for that matter the political and social conditions of the empire, did not exercise upon them some influence. But undoubted though it be that the Persian Mysteries underwent some modification in the Occident, the inadequacy of the data at our disposal prevents us from following this evolution in its various phases and from distinctly defining the local differences which it may have presented. All that we can do is to sketch in large outlines the character of the doctrines which were taught by it, indicating the additions and revisions which they apparently underwent. Besides, the alterations that it suffered were largely superficial. The identity of the images and hieratical formulas of the most remote periods and places, proves that before the time of its introduction into the Latin countries reformed Mazdaism had

already consolidated its theology. Contrary
to the ancient Græco-Roman paganism, which

MITHRAIC KRONOS (ÆON OR ZERVAN AKARANA) REPRESENTING BOUNDLESS TIME.

The statue here reproduced was found in the mithræum of Ostia before mentioned, where C. Valerius Heracles and his sons dedicated it in the year 190 A.D. This leontocephalous figure is entirely nude, the body being entwined six times by a serpent, the head of which rests on the skull of the god. Four wings decorated with the symbols of the seasons issue from the back. Each hand holds a key, and the right in addition a long scepter, the symbol of authority. A thunderbolt is engraved on the breast. On the base of the statue may be seen the hammer and tongs of Vulcan, the cock and the pine-cone consecrated to Æsculapius (or possibly to the Sun and to Attis), and the wand of Mercury—all

Fig. 20.

characteristic adjuncts of the Mithraic Saturn, and symbolizing the embodiment in him of the powers of all the gods. (*T. et M.*, p. 238.)

was an assemblage of practices and beliefs
without logical bond, Mithraism had a genuine

Fig. 21.
MITHRAIC KRONOS OF FLORENCE.
(*T. et M.*, p. 259.)

theology, a dogmatic system, which borrowed from science its fundamental principles.

The belief appears generally to prevail that

Mithra was the only Iranian god that was introduced into the Occident, and that everything in his religion that does not relate directly to him was adventitious and recent. This is a gratuitous and erroneous supposition. Mithra was accompanied in his migrations by a large representation from the Mazdean Pantheon, and if he was in the eyes of his devotees the principal hero of the religion to which he gave his name, he was nevertheless not its Supreme God.

At the pinnacle of the divine hierarchy and at the origin of things, the Mithraic theology, the heir of that of the Zervanitic Magi, placed boundless Time. Sometimes they would call it Αἰών or Sæculum, Κρόνος or Saturnus; but these appellations were conventional and contingent, for he was considered ineffable, bereft alike of name, sex, and passions. In imitation of his Oriental prototype, he was represented in the likeness of a human monster with the head of a lion and his body enveloped by a serpent. The multiplicity of attributes with which his statues are loaded is in keeping with the kaleidoscopic nature of his character. He bears the scepter and the bolts of divine sovereignty and holds in each hand a key as the monarch of the heavens whose portals he opens. His wings are symbolic of the rapidity of his flight. The reptile whose sinuous folds enwrap him, typifies the tortuous course of the Sun on the ecliptic; the signs of

Fig. 22.

MITHRAIC KRONOS (ÆON, OR INFINITE TIME).

Nude leontocephalous figure standing upright on a globe; in each hand a key; four wings; thrice entwined by a serpent, the head of which passes over the skull and is about to enter the mouth. Sketched by Bartoli from a description found in a mithræum discovered in the 16th century in Rome, between the Quirinal and the Viminal. (*T. et M.*, Fig. 21, p. 196.)

the zodiac engraved on his body and the emblems of the seasons that accompany them, are meant to represent the celestial and terrestrial phenomena that signalize the eternal flight of the years. He creates and destroys all things; he is the Lord and master of the four elements that compose the universe, he virtually unites in his person the power of all the gods, whom he alone has begotten. Sometimes he is identified with Destiny, at others with the primitive light or the primitive fire; while both conceptions rendered it possible for him to be compared with the Supreme Cause of the Stoics,—the heat which pervades all things, which has shaped all things, and which under another aspect was Fatality (Εἱμαρμένη). See Figs. 20-23; also Fig. 49.

The preachers of Mithra sought to resolve the grand problem of the origin of the world by the hypothesis of a series of successive generations. The first principle, according to an ancient belief found in India as well as in Greece, begot a primordial couple, the Heaven and the Earth; and the latter, impregnated by her brother, gave birth to the vast Ocean which was equal in power to its parents, and which appears to have formed with them the supreme triad of the Mithraic Pantheon. The relation of this triad to Kronos or Time from which it had sprung, was not clearly defined; and the starry Heavens of which the revolutions determined, as was believed, the course

Fig. 23.

MITHRAIC LEONTOCEPHALOUS KRONOS.

Bas-relief of white marble. Found in the same mithræum as the statue of Figure 22. Naked to the waist; the limbs clothed in wide trousers; the arms extended; and in each hand a torch. From the back four wings issue, two pointing upwards and two downwards, and around each is a serpent. Before the god is a circular burning altar, and from his mouth a band representing his breath extends to the fire of the altar. (*T. et M.*, Fig. 22, p. 196.)

of all events, appear at times to have been confounded with the eternal Destiny.

These three cosmic divinities were personified under other names less transparent. The
Heavens were naught less than Ormazd or
Jupiter, the Earth was identified with Speñta-
Armaîti or Juno, and the Ocean was similarly
called Apâm-Napât or Neptune. Like the
Greek theogonies, so the Mithraic traditions
narrated that Zeus succeeded Kronos, the king
of the first ages, in the government of the
world. The bas-reliefs show us this Mazdean
Saturn placing in the hands of his son the
thunderbolts which were the symbol of his
sovereign power. Henceforward Jupiter with
his consort Juno was to reign over all the
other gods, all of whom owe to this couple
their existence.

The Olympian deities were sprung in fact
from the marriage of the celestial Jupiter with
the terrestrial Juno. Their eldest daughter is
Fortune (*Fortuna primigenia*), who bestows
on her worshippers every grace of body and
every beauty of soul. Her beneficent generosity is contrasted with Anangke, which represents the unalterable rigor of fate. Themis
or the Law, the Moiræ or the Fates, were
other personifications of Destiny, which mani-
fests under various forms a character which
was susceptible of infinite development. The
sovereign couple further gave birth not only
to Neptune who became their peer, but to
a long line of other immortals: Artagnes
or Hercules, whose heroic deeds the sacred

hymns celebrated; Shahrîvar or Mars, who
was the god of the metals and succored the
pious warrior in his combats; Vulcan or Atar,
the genius of fire; Mercury, the messenger of
Zeus; Bacchus or Haoma, the personification
of the plant that furnished the sacred drink;
Silvanus or Drvâspa, protector of horses and
agriculture; then Anaïtis, the goddess of the
fecundating waters, who has been likened to
Venus and Cybele and who, presiding over
war, was also invoked under the name of
Minerva; Diana or Luna, who made the honey
which was used in the purifications; Vanaiñiti
or Nike, who gave victory to kings; Asha or
Arete, perfect virtue; and others besides.
This innumerable multitude of divinities was
enthroned with Jupiter or Zeus on the sun-
tipped summits of Mt. Olympus and composed the celestial court.

Contrasted with this luminous abode, where
dwelt the Most High gods in resplendent radiance, was a dark and dismal domain in the
bowels of the earth. Here Ahriman or Pluto,
born like Jupiter of Infinite Time, reigned with
Hecate over the maleficent monsters that had
issued from their impure embraces.

These demoniac confederates of the King of
Hell then ascended to the assault of Heaven
and attempted to dethrone the successor of
Kronos; but, shattered like the Greek giants
by the ruler of the gods, these rebel monsters
were hurled backward into the abyss from

Fig. 24.

FRAGMENTS OF A BAS-RELIEF IN WHITE ITALIAN MARBLE.

Found at Virunum, in Noricum, and now in the
Historical Museum Rudolfinum, Klagenfurt, Austria.
The central part of the monument is entirely destroyed; the head of the sun-god from the left-hand
corner alone having been left (see Fig. 11). The left
border represents a Hellenized illustration of Ahura-
Mazda's struggle with demons, after the manner of
the gigantomachy. The lower part of the same fragment exhibits the birth of Mithra. (*T. et M.*, p. 336.)

which they had risen (Figure 24). They made
their escape, however, from that place and
wandered about on the surface of the earth,
there to spread misery and to corrupt the
hearts of men, who, in order to ward off the
evils that menaced them, were obliged to appease these perverse spirits by offering them
expiatory sacrifices. The initiate also knew
how by appropriate rites and incantations to
enlist them in his service and to employ them
against the enemies whose destruction he was
meditating.

The gods no longer confined themselves to
the ethereal spheres which were their appa-
nage. If theogony represents them as gathered in Olympus around their parents and
sovereigns, cosmology exhibits them under
another aspect. Their energy filled the world,
and they were the active principles of its
transformations. Fire, personified in the
name of Vulcan, was the most exalted of these
natural forces, and it was worshipped in all
its manifestations, whether it shone in the stars
or in the lightning, whether it animated living creatures, stimulated the growth of plants,
or lay dormant in the bowels of the earth. In
the deep recesses of the subterranean crypts it
burned perpetually on the altars, and its votaries were fearful to contaminate its purity by
sacrilegious contact.

They opined with primitive artlessness that
fire and water were brother and sister, and

they entertained the same superstitious respect
for the one as for the other. They worshipped alike the saline floods which filled the
deep seas and which were termed indifferently Neptune and Oceanus, the springs that
gurgled from the recesses of the earth, the
rivers that flowed over its surface, and the
placid lakes resplendent in their limpid sheen.
A perpetual spring bubbled in the vicinity of
the temples, and was the recipient of the
homage and the offerings of its visitors. This
font perennial (*fons perennis*) was alike the
symbolization of the material and moral boons
that the inexhaustible generosity of Infinite
Time scattered throughout the universe, and
that of the spiritual rejuvenation accorded to
wearied souls in the eternity of felicity.

The primitive earth, the nourishing earth,
the mother earth (*terra mater*), fecundated by
the waters of Heaven, occupied a like important place, if not in the ritual, at least in the
doctrine of this religion; and the four cardinal
winds which were correlated with the deified
Seasons were invoked as genii to be both feared
and loved: feared because they were the
capricious arbiters of the temperature, which
brought heat or cold, tempests or calms,
which alternately moistened and dried the at-
mosphere, which produced the vegetation of the
spring and withered the foliage of the autumn,
—and loved as the diverse manifestations of
the air itself, which is the principle of all life.

In other words, Mithraism deified the four
simple bodies which, according to the physics
of the ancients, composed the universe. An
allegorical group, often reproduced, in which
a lion represented fire, a cup water, a serpent the earth, pictured the struggle of the
opposing elements, which were constantly
devouring one another and whose perpetual
transmutations and infinitely variable combinations provoked all the phenomena of nature
(Fig. 25).

Hymns of fantastic symbolism celebrated
the metamorphoses which the antitheses of
these four elements produced in the world.
The Supreme God drives a chariot drawn by
four steeds which turn ceaselessly round in a
fixed circle.   The first, which bears on its
shining coat the signs of the planets and constellations, is sturdy and agile and traverses
the circumference of the fixed circle with
extreme velocity;   the second, less vigorous
and less rapid in its movements, wears a
somber robe, of which one side only is illuminated by the rays of the sun;   the third pro-
ceeds more slowly still; and the fourth turns
slowly in the same spot, champing restlessly
its steel bit, whilst its companions move round
it as round a stationary column in the center.
The quadriga turns slowly and unimpeded, regularly completing its eternal course.   But at a
certain moment the fiery breath of the first
horse falling upon the fourth ignites its mane,

and its neighbor, exhausted by its efforts, in-
undates it with torrents of perspiration.   Fi-

Fig. 25.
GRAND MITHRAIC BAS-RELIEF OF HEDDERNHEIM,
GERMANY.

In the center Mithra with the two torch-bearers;
immediately above, the signs of the Zodiac; immediately above these, Mithra aiming his arrow at the rock
(page 138); below the bull a group composed of the
lion, the cup, and the servant.   For the obverse of this
bas-relief, see *supra*, p. 54.   (*T. et M.*, p. 364.)

nally, a still more remarkable phenomenon
takes place.   The appearance of the quartette

is transformed. The steeds interchange natures in such wise that the substance of all passes over to the most robust and ardent of the group, just as if a sculptor, after having modelled figures in wax, had borrowed the attributes of one to complete the others, and had ended by merging all into a single form. Then, the conquering steed in this divine struggle, having become by his triumph omnipotent, is identified with the charioteer himself. The first horse is the incarnation of fire or ether, the second of air, the third of water, and the fourth of the earth. The accidents which befall the last-mentioned horse, the earth, represent the conflagrations and inundations which have desolated and will in the future desolate our world; and the victory of the first horse is the symbolic image of the final conflict that shall destroy the existing order of all things.

The cosmic quadriga, which draws the suprasensible Cause, has not been figured in the sacred iconography. The latter reserved for a visible god this emblematic group. The votaries of Mithra, like the ancient Persians, adored the Sun that traversed each day in its chariot the spaces of the firmament and sank at dusk extinguishing its fires in the ocean. When it appeared again on the horizon, its brilliant light scattered in flight the spirits of darkness, and it purified all creation, to which its radiance restored life. A like worship was accorded to the Moon, which voyaged in the spheres above on a cart drawn by white bulls. The animal of reproduction and of agriculture had been assigned to the goddess that presided over the increase of plants and the generation of living creatures.

The elements, accordingly, were not the only natural bodies that were deified in the Mysteries. The two luminaries that fecundated nature were worshipped here the same as in primitive Mazdaism, but the conceptions which the Aryas formed of them have been profoundly transformed by the influences of Chaldæan theories.

As we have already said,* the ancient belief of the Persians had been forcibly subjected in Babylon to the influence of a theology which was based on the science of its day, and the majority of the gods of Iran had been likened to the stars worshipped in the valley of the Euphrates. They acquired thus a new character entirely different from their original one, and the name of the same deity thus assumed and preserved in the Occident a double meaning. The Magi were unsuccessful in harmonizing these new doctrines with their ancient religion, for the Semitic astrology was as irreconcilable with the naturalism of Iran as it was with the paganism of Greece. But looking upon these contradictions as simple differences of degree in the perception of one and

*See *supra*, page 10.

the same truth, the clergy reserved for the *élite* exclusively the revelation of the original Mazdean doctrines concerning the origin and destiny of man and the world, whilst the multitude were forced to remain content with the brilliant and superficial symbolism inspired by the speculations of the Chaldæans. The astronomical allegories concealed from the curiosity of the vulgar the real scope of the hieratic representations, and the promise of complete illumination, long withheld, fed the ardor of faith with the fascinating allurements of mystery.

The most potent of these sidereal deities, those which were most often invoked and for which were reserved the richest offerings, were the Planets. Conformably to astrological theories, the planets were endowed with virtues and qualities for which it is frequently difficult for us to discover adequate reasons. Each of the planetary bodies presided over a day of the week, to each some one metal was consecrated, each was associated with some one degree in the initiation, and their number has caused a special religious potency to be attributed to the number seven. In descending from the empyrean to the earth, the souls, it was thought, successively received from them their passions and qualities. These planetary bodies were frequently represented on the monuments, now by symbols recalling the elements of which they were formed or the sacrifices which were offered to them, and now under the aspect of the immortal gods throned on the Greek Olympus: Helios, Selene, Ares, Hermes, Zeus, Aphrodite, Kronos. But these images have here an entirely different signification from what they possess when they stand for Ahura-Mazda, Zervan, or the other gods of Mazdaism. Then the personifications of the Heavens or of Infinite Time are not seen in them, but only the luminous stars whose wandering course can be followed amid the constellations. This double system of interpretation was particularly applied to the Sun, conceived now as identical with Mithra and now as distinct from him. In reality there were two solar divinities in the Mysteries, one Iranian and the heir of the Persian Hvare, the other Semitic, the substitute of the Babylonian Shamash, identified with Mithra.

By the side of the planetary gods who have still a double character, purely sidereal divinities received their tribute of homage. The twelve signs of the Zodiac, which in their daily revolution subject creatures to their adverse influences, were represented in all of the mithræums under their traditional aspect (Fig. 26). Each of them was without doubt the object of particular veneration during the month over which it presided, and they were customarily grouped by threes according to the Seasons to which they conformed and with the worship of which theirs was associated. (See also Fig. 49.)

But the signs of the Zodiac were not the only constellations that were incorporated by the priests in their theology. The astronomical method of interpretation, having been

Fig. 26.

MARBLE BAS-RELIEF FOUND IN LONDON.

In the center the tauroctonous Mithra with the torch-bearers surrounded by the twelve signs of the Zodiac. In the lower corners busts of the Winds; in the upper corners the Sun on his quadriga and the Moon on a chariot drawn by bulls. The inscription reads: *Ulpius Silvanus emeritus leg(ionis) II Aug(ustae) votum solvit. Factus Arausione* (that is, honorably discharged at Orange). (*T. et M.*, p. 389.)

once adopted in the Mysteries, was freely extended and made to embrace all possible figures. There was scarcely any object or animal that was not in some way conceived as

the symbolic image of a stellar group. Thus
the raven, the cup, the dog, and the lion, that
ordinarily accompany the group of the tauroctonous Mithra, were readily identified with
the constellations of the same name. The
two celestial hemispheres that alternately pass
above and below the earth were personified
and likened to the Dioscuri, who, according to

Fig. 27.

MITHRAIC CAMEO.

After Chiflet, reproduced from C. W. King.

the Hellenic fable, lived and died by turns.
Mythology and erudition were everywhere
mingled. The hymns described a hero like
the Greek Atlas who bore on his untiring
shoulders the globe of Heaven, and who is
regarded as the inventor of astronomy. But
these demi-gods were relegated to the background; the planets and the signs of the
Zodiac never ceased to preserve their incon-
testable primacy, for it was they above all
others, according to the astrologers, that con-

trolled the existence of men and guided the course of things.

This was the capital doctrine that Babylon introduced into Mazdaism: belief in Fatality,

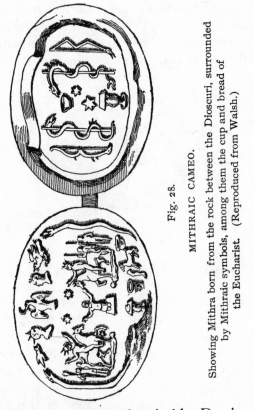

Fig. 28.

MITHRAIC CAMEO.

Showing Mithra born from the rock between the Dioscuri, surrounded by Mithraic symbols, among them the cup and bread of the Eucharist. (Reproduced from Walsh.)

the conception of an inevitable Destiny controlling the events of this world and inseparably conjoined with the revolution of the starry heavens. This Destiny, identified with Zervan, became the Supreme Being which engendered all things and ruled the universe. The development of the universe is subject to immutable laws and its various parts are united in the most intimate solidarity. The position of the planets, their mutual relations and energies, at every moment different, produce the series of terrestrial phenomena. Astrology, of which these postulates were the dogmas, certainly owes some share of its success to the Mithraic propaganda, and Mithraism is therefore partly responsible for the triumph in the West of this pseudo-science with its long train of errors and terrors.

The rigorous logic of its deductions assured to this stupendous chimera a more complete domination over reflecting minds than the belief in the infernal powers and in the invocation of spirits, although the latter commanded greater sway over popular credulity. The independent power attributed by Mazdaism to the principle of evil afforded justification for all manner of occult practices. Necromancy, oneiromancy, belief in the evil eye and in talismans, in witchcraft and conjurations, in fine, all the puerile and sinister aberrations of ancient paganism, found their justification in the rôle assigned to demons who incessantly interfered in the affairs of men. The Persian Mysteries are not free from the grave reproach of having condoned, if not of having really taught, these various superstitions. And the title "Magus" became in the popular mind, not without good reason, a synonym for "magician."

Yet neither the conception of an inexorable necessity unpityingly forcing the human race toward an unknown goal, nor even the fear of malevolent spirits bent on its destruction, was competent to attract the multitudes to the altars of the Mithraic gods. The rigor of these somber doctrines was tempered by a belief in benevolent powers sympathizing with the sufferings of mortals. Even the planets were not, as in the didactic works of the theoretical astrologists, cosmic powers whose favorable or sinister influence waxed great or diminished conformably to the revolutions of a circle fixed for all eternity. They were, as in the doctrine of the old Chaldæan religion, divinities that saw and heard, that rejoiced or lamented, whose wrath might be appeased, and whose favor might be gained by prayers and by offerings. The faithful reposed their confidence in the support of these benevolent protectors who combated without respite the powers of evil.

The hymns that celebrated the exploits of the gods have unfortunately almost all perished, and we know these epic traditions only through the monuments which served to illustrate them. Nevertheless, the character of this sacred poetry is recognizable in the *débris* which has come down to us. Thus, the labors

of Verethraghna, the Mazdean Hercules, were
chanted in Armenia. It is told here how he
strangled the dragons and aided Jupiter in his
triumphant combat with the monstrous giants;
and like the votaries of the Avesta, the
Roman adepts of Mazdaism compared him to
a bellicose and destructive boar.

But the hero that enjoyed the greatest rôle
in these warlike tales was Mithra. Certain
mighty deeds, which in the books of Zoroastrianism were attributed to other divinities,
were associated with his person. He had become the center of a cycle of legends which
alone explain the preponderant place that was
accorded him in this religion. It is because
of the astounding feats accomplished by him
that this god, who did not hold supreme rank
in the celestial hierarchy, has given his name
to the Persian Mysteries that were disseminated in the Occident.

For the ancient Magi, Mithra was, as we
have seen, the god of light, and as the light is
borne by the air he was thought to inhabit the
Middle Zone between Heaven and Hell, and
for this reason the name of μεσίτης was given
to him. In order to signalize this attribute in
the ritual, the sixteenth or middle day of each
month was consecrated to him. When he was
identified with Shamash,* his priests in invest-
ing him with the appellation of "intermediary"
doubtless had in mind the fact that, according

---

*See *supra*, page 10.

to the Chaldæan doctrines, the sun occupied
the middle place in the planetary choir. But
this middle position was not exclusively a
position in space; it was also invested with an
important moral significance.   Mithra was the

Fig. 29.

STATUES OF TORCH-BEARERS.

(Museum of Palermo.   *T. et M.*, p. 270.)

"mediator" between the unapproachable and
unknowable god that reigned in the ethereal
spheres and the human race that struggled
and suffered here below.   Shamash had already enjoyed analogous functions in Baby-

lon, and the Greek philosophers also saw in the glittering globe that poured down upon this world its light, the ever-present image of the invisible Being, of whom reason alone could conceive the existence.

It was in this adventitious quality of the genius of the solar light that Mithra was best known in the Occident, and his monuments frequently suggest this borrowed character. It was customary to represent him between two youthful figures, one with an uplifted, the other with an inverted, torch. These youths bore the enigmatic epithets of *Cauti* and *Cautopati*, and were naught else than the double incarnation of his person (Figs. 18 and 29). These two dadophori, as they were called, and the tauroctonous hero formed together a triad, and in this "triple Mithra" was variously seen either the star of day, whose coming at morn the cock announced, who passed at midday triumphantly into the zenith and at night languorously fell toward the horizon; or the sun which, as it waxed in strength, entered the constellation of Taurus and marked the beginning of spring,—the sun whose conquering ardors fecundated nature in the heart of summer and the sun that afterwards, enfeebled, traversed the sign of the Scorpion and announced the return of winter. From another point of view, one of these torchbearers was regarded as the emblem of heat and of life, and the other as the emblem of

cold and of death. Similarly, the tauroctonous group was variously explained with the
aid of an astronomical symbolism more ingenious than rational. Yet these sidereal interpretations were nothing more than intellectual
diversions designed to amuse the neophytes

Fig. 30.

MITHRA BORN FROM THE ROCK.

Bas-relief found in the crypt of St. Clements at Rome.
(*T. et M.*, p. 202.)

prior to their receiving the revelation of the
esoteric doctrines that constituted the ancient
Iranian legend of Mithra. The story of this
legend is lost, but the bas-reliefs recount
certain episodes of it, and its contents appear
to have been somewhat as follows:

The light bursting from the heavens, which

were conceived as a solid vault, became, in the mythology of the Magi, Mithra born from the rock. The tradition ran that the "Generative Rock," of which a standing image was worshipped in the temples, had given birth to Mithra on the banks of a river, under the

Fig. 31.

MITHRA BORN FROM THE ROCK.

Holding in his hand the Grape which in the West replaced the Haoma of the Persians. (*T. et M.*, p. 231.)

shade of a sacred tree, and that shepherds alone,* ensconced in a neighboring mountain, had witnessed the miracle of his entrance into the world. They had seen him issue forth from the rocky mass, his head adorned with a Phrygian cap, armed with a knife, and carry-

*See the lower part of Fig. 24.

ing a torch that had illuminated the somber depths below (Fig. 30). Worshipfully the shepherds drew near, offering the divine infant the first fruits of their flock and their harvests. But the young hero was naked and exposed to the winds that blew with violence: he had concealed himself in the branches of a fig-tree, and detaching the fruit from the tree with the aid of his knife, he ate of it, and stripping it of its leaves he made himself garments. Thus equipped for the battle, he was able henceforward to measure his strength with the other powers that peopled the marvellous world into which he had entered. For although the shepherds were pasturing their flocks when he was born, all these things came to pass before there were men on earth.

The god with whom Mithra first measured his strength was the Sun. The latter was compelled to render homage to the superiority of his rival and to receive from him his investiture. His conqueror placed upon his head the radiant crown that he has borne in his daily course ever since his downfall. Then he caused him to rise again, and extending to him his right hand concluded with him a solemn covenant of friendship. And ever after, the two allied heroes faithfully supported each other in all their enterprises (Fig. 32).

The most extraordinary of these epic adventures was Mithra's combat with the bull, the first living creature created by Ormazd. This

Fig. 32.

FRAGMENT OF THE BAS-RELIEF OF VIRUNUM.

Showing scenes from the life of Mithra. Among them Mithra crowning the sun-god with a radiate halo, his ascension in the solar chariot to Heaven, and his smiting the rock from which the waters flowed. (*T. et M.*, p. 336.)

ingenious fable carries us back to the very be-
ginnings of civilization. It could never have
risen save among a people of shepherds and

Fig. 33.

THE TAUROCTONOUS (BULL-SLAYING) MITHRA AND
THE TAUROPHOROUS (BULL-BEARING) MITHRA;
BETWEEN THEM THE DOG.

Clay cup found at Lanuvium. (*T. et M.*, Fig. 80, p. 247.)

hunters with whom cattle, the source of all
wealth, had become an object of religious

veneration.   In the eyes of such a people, the capture of a wild bull was an achievement so highly fraught with honor as to be apparently no derogation even for a god.

The redoubtable bull was grazing in a pasture on the mountain-side; the hero, resorting to a bold stratagem, seized it by the horns and succeeded in mounting it.   The infuriated quadruped, breaking into a gallop, struggled in vain to free itself from its rider; the latter, although unseated by the bull's mad rush, never for a moment relaxed his hold; he suffered himself to be dragged along, suspended from the horns of the animal, which, finally exhausted by its efforts, was forced to surrender.   Its conqueror then seizing it by its hind hoofs, dragged it backwards over a road strewn with obstacles (Fig. 33) into the cave which served as his home.

This painful Journey (*Transitus*) of Mithra became the symbol of human sufferings.   But the bull, it would appear, succeeded in making its escape from its prison, and roamed again at large over the mountain pastures.   The Sun then sent the raven, his messenger, to carry to his ally the command to slay the fugitive.   Mithra received this cruel mission much against his will, but submitting to the decree of Heaven he pursued the truant beast with his agile dog, succeeded in overtaking it just at the moment when it was taking refuge in the cave which it had quitted, and seizing it by the nostrils with one hand, with the other he plunged deep into its flank his hunting-knife.

Then came an extraordinary prodigy to pass.

Fig. 34.

TWO BRONZE PLAQUES (VATICAN).

The one to the left has the head of Jupiter (Silvanus?). The right hand holds a pine-cone, the left a branch entwined by a serpent. On the right shoulder is an eagle, and the breast is decorated with Mithraic figures in relief: the tauroctonous Mithra, a cup, the head of a ram, and a five-rayed disc. The right-hand bust is that of a bearded Oriental with Phrygian cap, holding in the right hand a pine-cone and in the left a torch entwined by a serpent—a crude piece of work and probably of Asiatic origin. (*T. et M.*, Figs. 97 and 98, p. 260.)

From the body of the moribund victim sprang all the useful herbs and plants that cover the earth with their verdure. From the spinal cord of the animal sprang the wheat that gives us our bread, and from its blood the vine that produces the sacred drink of the Mysteries. In vain did the Evil Spirit launch forth his unclean demons against the anguish-wrung animal, in order to poison in it the very sources of life; the scorpion, the ant, the serpent, strove in vain to consume the genital parts and to drink the blood of the prolific quadruped; but they were powerless to impede the miracle that was enacting. The seed of the bull, gathered and purified by the Moon, produced all the different species of useful animals, and its soul, under the protection of the dog, the faithful companion of Mithra, ascended into the celestial spheres above, where, receiving the honors of divinity, it became under the name of Silvanus the guardian of herds. Thus, through the sacrifice which he had so resignedly undertaken, the taurocto-nous hero became the creator of all the beneficent beings on earth; and, from the death which he had caused, was born a new life, more rich and more fecund than the old.

Meanwhile, the first human couple had been called into existence, and Mithra was charged with keeping a watchful eye over this privileged race. It was in vain the Spirit of Darkness invoked his pestilential scourges to destroy it; the god always knew how to balk his mortiferous designs. Ahriman first desolated the land by causing a protracted drought, and its inhabitants, tortured by thirst, implored the

aid of his ever-victorious adversary. The divine archer discharged his arrows against a
precipitous rock, and there gushed forth from
it a spring of living water to which the sup-
pliants thronged to cool their parched palates.*
But a still more terrible cataclysm followed,
which menaced all nature. A universal deluge depopulated the earth, which was over-
whelmed by the waters of the rivers and the
seas. One man alone, secretly advised by the
gods, had constructed a boat and had saved
himself, together with his cattle, in an ark
which floated on the broad expanse of waters.
Then a great conflagration ravaged the world
and consumed utterly both the habitations
of men and of beasts. But the creatures of
Ormazd also ultimately escaped this new peril,
thanks to celestial protection, and henceforward the human race was permitted to wax
great and multiply in peace.

The heroic period of history was now closed,
and the terrestrial mission of Mithra accomplished. In a Last Supper, which the initiated
commemorated by mystical love feasts, he
celebrated with Helios and the other companions of his labors the termination of their common struggles. Then the gods ascended to
the Heavens. Borne by the Sun on his radiant
quadriga, Mithra crossed the Ocean, which
sought in vain to engulf him (Fig. 35), and
took up his habitation with the rest of the im-

*See *supra*, p. 117, Fig. 25, and *infra*, p. 196, Fig. 45.

Fig. 35.

BAS-RELIEF OF APULUM, DACIA.

In the center, the tauroctonous Mithra with the
two torch-bearers; to the left, Mithra mounted on the
bull, and Mithra taurophorous; to the right, a lion
stretched lengthwise above a cup (symbols of fire and
water). Upper border: Bust of Luna; new-born
Mithra reclining near the banks of a stream; shepherd
standing, with lambs; bull in a hut and bull in a boat;
underneath, the seven altars; Mithra drawing a bow;
bust of the Sun. Lower border: Banquet of Mithra
and the Sun; Mithra mounting the quadriga of the
Sun; the Ocean surrounded by a serpent. (*T. et M.*,
p. 309.)

mortals. But from the heights of Heaven he never ceased to protect the faithful ones that piously served him.

This mythical recital of the origin of the world enables us to understand the importance which the tauroctonous god enjoyed in his religion, and to comprehend better what the pagan theologians endeavored to express by the title "mediator." Mithra is the creator to whom Jupiter-Ormazd committed the task of establishing and of maintaining order in nature. He is, to speak in the philosophical language of the times, the Logos that emanated from God and shared His omnipotence; who, after having fashioned the world as demiurge, continued to watch faithfully over it. The primal defeat of Ahriman had not reduced him to absolute impotence; the struggle between the good and the evil was still conducted on earth between the emissaries of the sovereign of Olympus and those of the Prince of Darkness; it raged in the celestial spheres in the opposition of propitious and adverse stars, and it reverberated in the hearts of men,—the epitomes of the universe.

Life is a battle, and to issue forth from it victorious the law must be faithfully fulfilled that the divinity himself revealed to the ancient Magi. What were the obligations that Mithraism imposed upon its followers? What were those "commandments" to which its adepts had to bow in order to be rewarded in the world to come? Our incertitude on these points is extreme, for we have not the shadow of a right to identify the precepts revealed in the Mysteries with those formulated in the Avesta. Nevertheless, it would appear certain that the ethics of the Magi of the Occident had made no concession to the license of the Babylonian cults and that it had still preserved the lofty character of the ethics of the ancient Persians. Perfect purity had remained for them the cult toward which the life of the faithful should tend. Their ritual required repeated lustrations and ablutions, which were believed to wash away the stains of the soul. This catharsis or purification both conformed to the Mazdean traditions and was in harmony with the general tendencies of the age. Yielding to these tendencies, the Mithraists carried their principles even to excess, and their ideals of perfection verged on asceticism. Abstinence from certain foods and absolute continence were regarded as praiseworthy.

Resistance to sensuality was one of the aspects of the combat with the principle of evil. To support untiringly this combat with the followers of Ahriman, who, under multiple forms, disputed with the gods the empire of the world, was the duty of the servitors of Mithra. Their dualistic system was particularly adapted to fostering individual effort and to developing human energy. They did not lose themselves, as did the other sects, in contemplative mysticism; for them, the good dwelt in action. They rated strength higher than gentleness, and preferred courage to lenity. From their long association with barbaric religions, there was perhaps a residue of

Fig. 36.

VOTIVE INSCRIPTION TO MITHRA NABARZE
(VICTORIOUS).

Found at Sarmizegetusa. (*T. et M.*, p. 281.)

cruelty in their ethics. A religion of soldiers, Mithraism exalted the military virtues above all others.

In the war which the zealous champion of piety carries on unceasingly with the malign demons, he is assisted by Mithra. Mithra is the god of help, whom one never invokes in vain, an unfailing haven, the anchor of salvation for mortals in all their trials, the dauntless champion who sustains his devotees in their frailty, through all the tribulations of life. As with the Persians, so here he is still the defender of truth and justice, the protector of holiness, and the intrepid antagonist of the powers of darkness. Eternally young and vigorous, he pursues them without mercy; "always awake, always alert," it is impossible to surprise him; and from his never-ceasing combats he always emerges the victor. This is the idea that unceasingly occurs in the inscriptions, the idea expressed by the Persian surname *Nabarze* (Fig. 36), by the Greek and Latin epithets of ἀνίκητος, *invictus*, *insuperabilis*. As the god of armies, Mithra caused his *protégés* to triumph over their barbarous adversaries, and likewise in the moral realm he gave them victory over the instincts of evil, inspired by the Spirit of Falsehood, and he assured them salvation both in this world and in that to come.

Like all the Oriental cults, the Persian Mysteries mingled with their cosmogonic fables and their theological speculations, ideas of deliverance and redemption. They believed in the conscious survival after death of the divine essence that dwells within us, and in punishments and rewards beyond the tomb.

The souls, of which an infinite multitude peopled the habitations of the Most High, descended here below to animate the bodies of men, either because they were compelled by bitter necessity to fall into this material and corrupt world, or because they had dropped of their own accord upon the earth to undertake here the battle against the demons. When after death the genius of corruption took possession of the body, and the soul quitted its human prison, the devas of darkness and the emissaries of Heaven disputed for its possession. A special decree decided whether it was worthy to ascend again into Paradise. If it was stained by an impure life, the emissaries of Ahriman dragged it down to the infernal depths, where they inflicted upon it a thousand tortures; or perhaps, as a mark of its fall, it was condemned to take up its abode in the body of some unclean animal. If, on the contrary, its merits outweighed its faults, it was borne aloft to the regions on high.

The heavens were divided into seven spheres, each of which was conjoined with a planet. A sort of ladder, composed of eight superposed gates, the first seven of which were constructed of different metals, was the symbolic suggestion in the temples, of the road to be followed to reach the supreme region of the fixed stars. To pass from one story to the next, each time the wayfarer had to enter a gate guarded by an angel of Ormazd. The initiates alone, to whom the appropriate formulas had been taught, knew how to appease these inexorable guardians. As the soul traversed these different zones, it rid itself, as one would of garments, of the passions and faculties that it had received in its descent to the earth. It abandoned to the Moon its vital and nutritive energy, to Mercury its desires, to Venus its wicked appetites, to the Sun its intellectual capacities, to Mars its love of war, to Jupiter its ambitious dreams, to Saturn its inclinations. It was naked, stripped of every vice and every sensibility, when it penetrated the eighth heaven to enjoy there, as an essence supreme, and in the eternal light that bathed the gods, beatitude without end.*

It was Mithra, the protector of truth, that presided over the judgment of the soul after its decease. It was he, the mediator, that served as a guide to his faithful ones in their courageous ascent to the empyrean; he was the celestial father that received them in his resplendent mansion, like children who had returned from a distant voyage.

The happiness reserved for these quintessentialized monads in a spiritual world is rather difficult to conceive, and doubtless this doctrine had but feeble attraction for vulgar

*This Mithraic doctrine has recently been compared with other analogous beliefs and studied in detail by M. Bossuet. "Die Himmelreise der Seele" (*Archiv für Religionswissenschaft*, Vol. IV., 1901, p. 160 ff.).

minds.   Another belief, which was added to
the first by a sort of superfœtation, offered the
prospect of more material enjoyment.   The
doctrine of the immortality of the soul was
rounded off by the doctrine of the resurrection
of the flesh.

The struggle between the principles of good
and evil is not destined to continue into all
eternity.   When the age assigned for its dura-
tion shall have rolled away, the scourges sent
by Ahriman will compass the destruction of
the world.   A marvellous bull, analogous to
the primitive bull, will then again appear on
earth, and Mithra will redescend and reawaken
men to life.   All will sally forth from the
tombs, will assume their former appearance,
and recognize one another.   Humanity entire
will unite in one grand assembly, and the god
of truth will separate the good from the bad.
Then in a supreme sacrifice he will immolate
the divine bull; will mingle its fat with the
consecrated wine, and will offer to the just this
miraculous beverage which will endow them
all with immortality.   Then Jupiter-Ormazd,
yielding to the prayers of the beatified ones,
will cause to fall from the heavens a devouring fire which will annihilate all the wicked.
The defeat of the Spirit of Darkness will be
achieved, and in the general conflagration
Ahriman and his impure demons will perish
and the rejuvenated universe enjoy unto all
eternity happiness without end.

We who have never experienced the Mithraic spirit of grace are apt to be disconcerted by the incoherence and absurdity of this body of doctrine, such as it has been shown forth in our reconstruction. A theology at once naïve and artificial here combines primitive myths, the naturalistic tendency of which is still transparent, with an astrological system whose logical structure only serves to render its radical falsity all the more palpable. All the impossibilities of the ancient polytheistic fables here subsist side by side with philosophical speculations on the evolution of the universe and the destiny of man. The discordance between tradition and reflection is extremely marked here and it is augmented by the contrariety between the doctrine of fatalism and that of the efficacy of prayer and the need of worship. But this religion, like any other, must not be estimated by its metaphysical verity. It would ill become us to-day to dissect the cold corpse of this faith in order to ascertain its inward organic vices. The important thing is to understand how Mithraism lived and grew great, and why it failed to win the empire of the world.

Its success was in great part undoubtedly due to the vigor of its ethics, which above all things favored action. In an epoch of anarchy and emasculation, its mystics found in its precepts both stimulus and support. The conviction that the faithful ones formed part of a

sacred army charged with sustaining with the
Principle of Good the struggle against the
power of evil, was singularly adapted to pro-
voking their most pious efforts and transform-
ing them into ardent zealots.

The Mysteries exerted another powerful influence, also, in fostering some of the most
exalted aspirations of the human soul: the
desire for immortality and the expectation of
final justice. The hopes of life beyond the
tomb which this religion instilled in its votaries were one of the secrets of its power in
these troublous times, when solicitude for the
life to come disturbed all minds.

But several other sects offered to their
adepts just as consoling prospects of a future
life. The special attraction of Mithraism
dwelt, therefore, in other qualities of its doc-
trinal system. Mithraism, in fact, satisfied
alike both the intelligence of the educated and
the hearts of the simple-minded. The apotheosis of Time as First Cause and that of the
Sun, its physical manifestation, which maintained on earth heat and light, were highly
philosophical conceptions. The worship rendered to the Planets and to the Constellations,
the course of which determined terrestrial
events, and to the four Elements, whose infinite combinations produced all natural phenomena, is ultimately reducible to the worship
of the principles and agents recognized by
ancient science, and the theology of the Mys-

teries was, in this respect, nothing but the religious expression of the physics and astronomy
of the Roman world.

This theoretical conformity of revealed dogmas with the accepted ideas of science was
calculated to allure cultivated minds, but it had
no hold whatever upon the ignorant souls of
the populace. These, on the other hand, were
eminently amenable to the allurements of a
doctrine that deified the whole of physical and
tangible reality. The gods were everywhere,
and they mingled in every act of life; the fire
that cooked the food and warmed the bodies
of the faithful, the water that allayed their
thirst and cleansed their persons, the very air
that they breathed, and the light that illuminated their paths, were the objects of their
adoration. Perhaps no other religion ever
offered to its sectaries in a higher degree than
Mithraism opportunities for prayer and motives for veneration. When the initiated be-
took himself in the evening to the sacred
grotto concealed in the solitude of the forests,
at every step new sensations awakened in his
heart some mystical emotion. The stars that
shone in the sky, the wind that whispered in
the foliage, the spring or brook that babbled
down the mountain-side, even the earth that
he trod under his feet, were in his eyes divine,
and all surrounding nature provoked in him a
worshipful fear for the infinite forces that
swayed the universe.

THE MITHRAIC LITURGY, CLERGY AND
DEVOTEES

IN ALL the religions of classical antiquity
there is one feature which, while formerly
very conspicuous and perhaps the most important of all for the faithful, has to-day almost totally disappeared. It is their liturgy.
The Mysteries of Mithra form no exception to
this unfortunate rule. The sacred books which
contain the prayers recited or chanted during
the services, the ritual of the initiations, and
the ceremonials of the feasts, have vanished
and left scarce a trace behind. A verse borrowed from one unknown hymn is almost all
that has come down to us from the collections
which anciently must have been so abundant.
The old Gâthas composed in honor of the
Mazdean gods were translated into Greek
during the Alexandrian epoch, and Greek remained for a long time the language of the
Mithraic cult, even in the Occident. Barbaric
words, incomprehensible to the profane, were
interspersed throughout the sacred texts and
augmented the veneration of the worshippers
for the ancient formulary, as well as their confidence in its efficacy. Such were the epithets
like *Nabarze*, "victorious," which has been applied to Mithra, or the obscure invocations

like *Nama, Nama Sebesio,* engraved on our bas-reliefs, which have never yet been inter-

Fig. 37.

TAUROCTONOUS MITHRA. BAS-RELIEF OF WHITE MARBLE (BOLOGNA).

Important for its accessory figures. In the center, the dog, serpent, scorpion, the two torch-bearers, and above the one to the left the raven. Near each torch-bearer is a pine-tree (?). On the upper border are the busts of the seven planets in the following order from the left: The Sun, Saturn, Venus, Jupiter, Hermes, Mars, and Luna. The lower border, three figures at a banquet; infant, or Eros (?); bearded figure reclining (Oceanus). (*T. et M.*, Fig. 99, p. 261.)

preted. A scrupulous respect for the traditional practices of their sect characterized the Magi of Asia Minor, and continued to be manifested with unabated ardor among their Latin successors. On the downfall of paganism, the latter still took pride in worshipping the gods according to the ancient Persian rites which Zoroaster was said to have instituted. These rites sharply distinguished their religion from all the others that were practised at the same time in Rome, and prevented its Persian origin from ever being forgotten.

If some piece of good fortune should one day unearth for us a Mithraic missal, we should be able to study there these ancient usages and to participate in imagination in the celebration of the services. Deprived as we are of this indispensable guide, we are excluded utterly from the sanctuary and know the esoteric discipline of the Mysteries only from a few indiscretions. A text of St. Jerome, confirmed by a series of inscriptions, informs us that there were seven degrees of initiation and that the mystic (μύστης, *sacratus*) successively assumed the names of Raven (*corax*), Occult (*cryphius*), Soldier (*miles*), Lion (*leo*), Persian (*Perses*), Runner of the Sun (*heliodromus*), and Father (*pater*). These strange appellations were not empty epithets with no practical bearing. On certain occasions the celebrants donned garbs suited to the title that had been accorded them. On the bas-reliefs we see them carrying the counterfeit heads of animals, of soldiers, and of Persians. (See Fig. 38, p. 159) "Some flap their wings like birds, imitating the cry of crows; others growl like lions," says a Christian writer of the fourth century;* "in such manner are they that are called wise basely travestied."

These sacred masks, of which the ecclesias· tical writer exhibits the ridiculous side, were interpreted by pagan theologians as an allusion to the signs of the Zodiac, and even to the doctrine of metempsychosis. Such divergences of interpretation simply prove that the real meaning of these animal disguises was no longer understood. They are in reality a survival of primitive practices which have left their traces in numerous cults. We find the titles of Bear, Ox, Colt, and other similar names borne by the initiates of the different Mysteries in Greece and Asia Minor. They go back to that prehistoric period where the divinities themselves were represented under the forms of animals; and when the worshipper, in taking the name and semblance of his gods, believed that he identified himself with them. The lion-headed Kronos having become the incarnation of Time, was substituted for the lions which the forerunners of the Mithraists worshipped; and similarly the cloth and paper masks with which the Roman mystics covered their faces were substitutes for the animal skins with which their barbarous predecessors originally clothed themselves, be it that they believed they thus

---

*Ps. Augustine, *Quaest. vet. et novi Test.*, (*T. et M.*, Vol. II., p. 8).

entered into communion with the monstrous idols which they worshipped, or that, in enveloping themselves in the pelts of their flayed victims, they conceived these bloody tunics to possess some purifying virtue.

To the primitive titles of Raven and Lion others were afterward added for the purpose of attaining the sacred number seven. The seven degrees of initiation through which the mystic was forced to pass in order to acquire perfect wisdom and purity, answered to the seven planetary spheres which the soul was forced to traverse in order to reach the abode of the blessed.* After having been Raven, the initiates were promoted to the rank of Occult ($\kappa\rho\acute{v}\phi\iota\sigma$). The members of this class, hidden by some veil, probably remained invisible to the rest of the congregation. To exhibit them (*ostendere*) constituted a solemn act. The Soldier (*miles*) formed part of the sacred militia of the invincible god and waged war under his directions on the powers of evil. The dignity of Persian recalled the first origin of the Mazdean religion, and he who obtained it assumed during the sacred ceremonies the Oriental custom of donning the Phrygian cap, which had also been bestowed on Mithra. The latter having been identified with the Sun, his servitors invested themselves with the name of Runners of the Sun ($\mathrm{'H}\lambda\iota\sigma\delta\rho\acute{\sigma}\mu\sigma\iota$); lastly, the title "Fathers" was borrowed from the Greek

*See *supra*, p. 144.

Thiasi, where this honorific appellation frequently designated the directors of the community.

In this septuple division of the deities, certain additional distinctions were established.
We may conclude from a passage in Porphyry
that the taking of the first three degrees did
not authorize participation in the Mysteries.
These initiates, comparable to the Christian
catechumens, were the Servants (ὑπηρετοῦντες).
To enter this order it was sufficient to have
been admitted to the Ravens, doubtless so
called because mythology made the raven the
servitor of the Sun. Only the mystics that had
received the Leontics became Participants
(μετέχοντες), and it is for this reason that the
grade of *Leo* is mentioned more frequently in
the inscriptions than any other. Finally, at
the summit of the hierarchy were placed the
Fathers, who appear to have presided over
the sacred ceremonies (*pater sacrorum*) and to
have commanded the other classes of the
faithful. The head of the Fathers themselves
bore the name of *Pater Patrum*, sometimes
transformed into *Pater patratus*, in order to
introduce an official sacerdotal title into a sect
which had become Roman. These grand-
masters of the adepts retained until their death
the general direction of the cult. The reverence and affection which were entertained for
these venerable dignitaries are indicated by
their name of Father, and the mystics placed

under their authority were called brethren by
one another, because the fellow-initiates (*con-
sacranei*) were expected to cherish mutual affection.*

Admission (*acceptio*) to the lower orders could
be accorded even to children. We do not
know whether the initiates were obliged to
remain in any one of the grades for a fixed
length of time. The Fathers probably decided
when the novice was sufficiently prepared to
receive the higher initiation, which they conferred in person (*tradere*).

This ceremony of initiation appears to have
borne the name of sacrament (*sacramentum*),
doubtless because of the oath which the neophyte took and which was compared to that
made by the conscripts enrolled in the army.
The candidate engaged above all things not to
divulge the doctrines and the rites revealed to
him, but other and more special vows were
exacted of him. Thus, the mystic that aspired
to the title of *Miles* was presented with a
crown on a sword. He thrust it back with his
hand and caused it to fall on his shoulder, say-
ing that Mithra was his only crown. There-
after, he never wore one, neither at banquets
nor when it was awarded to him as a military
honor, replying to the person who conferred
it: "It belongs to my god," that is to say, to
the invincible god.

We are as poorly acquainted with the liturgy

*See *infra*, p. 190, footnote.

of the seven Mithraic sacraments as we are with the dogmatic instructions that accompanied them. We know, however, that conformably to the ancient Iranian rites, repeated ablutions were prescribed to neophytes as a kind of baptism designed to wash away their guilty stains. As with a certain class of Gnostics, this lustration doubtless had different effects at each stage of initiation, and it might consist according to circumstances either in a simple sprinkling of holy water, or in an actual immersion as in the cult of Isis.

Tertullian also compared the confirmation of his co-religionists to the ceremony in which they "signed" the forehead of the soldier. It appears, however, that the sign or seal impressed was not, as in the Christian liturgy, an unction, but a mark burned with a red-hot iron like that applied in the army to recruits before they were admitted to the oath. This indelible imprint perpetuated the memory of the solemn engagement by which the person under vow contracted to serve in that order of chivalry which Mithraism constituted. On reception among the Lions, there were new purifications. But this animal being the emblem of the principle of fire, the use of water, the element hostile to fire, was renounced; and, in order to preserve the initiate from the blemish of sin, honey was poured on his hands and applied to his tongue, as was the custom with new-born children. It was honey also

that was presented to the Persian because of
its preservative virtue, as Porphyry tells us;*
in fact, marvellous properties appear to have
been associated with this substance, which was
believed to have been produced under the influence of the moon.   According to the ancient
ideas, it was the food of the blessed, and its
absorption by the neophyte made him a peer
of the gods.†

In the Mazdean service, the celebrant consecrated the bread and the water which he
mingled with the intoxicating juice of the
Haoma prepared by him, and he consumed
these foods during the performance of his sacrifice. These ancient usages were preserved
in the Mithraic initiations, save that for the
Haoma, a plant unknown in the Occident, was
substituted the juice of the vine. A loaf of
bread and a goblet of water were placed before
the mystic, over which the priest pronounced
the sacred formula. This oblation of bread
and water, with which undoubtedly wine was
afterward mixed, is compared by the apologists to the Christian sacrament of the Lord's
Supper. Like the latter, it was not granted
until after a long novitiate. It is probable
that only those initiates who had attained the
degree of Lions were admitted to it, and that
this is the reason that the name of "Partici-

---

*Porph., *De antro nymph.*, c. 15 (*T. et M.*, Vol. II., p. 40).

†The liturgic use of honey has recently been elucidated by
Usener, "Milch und Honig" (*Hermes*, LVII), 1902, p. 177 ff.

Fig. 38.

MITHRAIC COMMUNION.

At the left the Raven and the Persian; at the right, the Soldier and the Lion. (Fragment of a bas-relief recently discovered in Konjica, Bosnia.) (*T. et M., Introduction,* p. 175.)

pants" was given to them. A curious bas-relief recently published shows us the spectacle of this sacred repast (Fig. 38). Before two persons stretched upon a couch covered with pillows is placed a tripod bearing four tiny loaves of bread, each marked with a cross. Around them are grouped the initiates of the different orders, and one of them, the Persian, presents to the two a drinking-horn; whilst a second vessel is held in the hands of one of the Participants. These love feasts are evidently the ritual commemoration of the banquet which Mithra celebrated with the Sun before his ascension.* From this mystical banquet, and especially from the imbibing of the sacred wine, supernatural effects were expected. The intoxicating liquor gave not only vigor of body and material prosperity, but wisdom of mind; it communicated to the neophyte the power to combat the malignant spirits, and what is more, conferred upon him as upon his god a glorious immortality.

The sacramental collation was accompanied, or rather preceded, by other rites of a different character. These were genuine trials imposed upon the candidate. To receive the sacred ablutions and the consecrated food, the Participant was obliged to prepare for them by prolonged abstinence and numerous austerities; he played the rôle of sufferer in certain dramatic expiations of strange character and

*See above, p. 138

of which we know neither the number nor
the succession. If we can believe a Christian
writer of the fourth century,* the eyes of the
neophyte were bandaged, his hands were bound
with the entrails of chickens, and he was compelled to leap over a ditch filled with water;
finally, a liberator approached with a sword
and sundered his loathsome bonds. Sometimes, the terrified mystic took part, if not as
an actor, at least as a spectator, in a simulated
murder, which in its origin was undoubtedly
real. In late periods, the officiants were contented with producing a sword dipped in the
blood of a man who had met a violent death.
The cruelty of these ceremonies, which among
the warlike tribes of the Taurus must have
been downright savage orgies, was softened
by contact with western civilization. In any
event, they had become more fear-inspiring
than fearful, and it was the moral courage of
the initiate that was tried rather than his physical endurance. The idea which was sought
to be attained was the stoic "apathy," the
absence of every sensitive emotion. The
atrocious tortures, the impossible macerations,
to which some too credulous or inventive
authors have condemned the adepts of the
Mysteries, must be relegated to the realm of
fable, as must likewise the pretended human
sacrifices which were said to have been perpetrated in the shades of the sacred crypts.

*See above, p. 153, footnote.

Nevertheless, it must not be supposed that
Mithraism exhibited nothing more than the
benignant phantasmagoria of a species of ancient freemasonry. There had subsisted in
its liturgic drama vestiges of its original bar-
barism, of the time when in the forests, in the
depths of some dark cave, corybantes, enveloped in the skins of beasts, sprinkled the altars
with their blood. In the Roman towns, the
secluded caverns of the mountains were replaced by subterranean vaults (*spelæa*) of far
less imposing aspect (Fig. 39). But even in
these artificial grottos the scenes of initiation
were calculated to produce on the neophyte
a profound impression. When, after having
traversed the approaches of the temple, he
descended the stairs of the crypt, he perceived
before him in the brilliantly decorated and
illuminated sanctuary the venerated image of
the tauroctonous Mithra erected in the apse,
then the monstrous statues of the leontocephalous Kronos, laden with attributes and
mystic symbols, the meaning of which was
still unknown to him. At the two sides, partly
in the shadow, the assistants, kneeling on
stone benches, were seen praying. Lamps
ranged about the choir threw their bright
rays on the images of the gods and the celebrants, who, robed in strange costumes, received the new convert. Fitful flashes of light
skillfully manipulated impressed his eyes and
his mind. The sacred emotion with which he

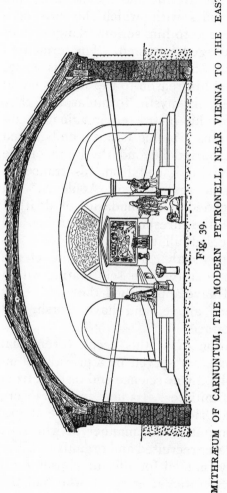

Fig. 39.

MITHRÆUM OF CARNUNTUM, THE MODERN PETRONELL, NEAR VIENNA TO THE EAST.

(Restored by Tragan.)

This mithræum, like all others of the same style, is underground. Before the great bas-relief of Mithra slaying the bull are two altars, the one large and square in form, the other smaller and richly ornamented. The small statue on the left is Mithra being born from the rock. At the right of the entrance we see the lion of Mithra and at the left a font for holy water. The two torch-bearers stand on the pillars which separate the aisles. The mithræum is approached by a stairway and through a square hall (or pronaos) which is considerably larger than the sanctum itself. (*T. et M*, p. 493).

was seized lent to images which were really puerile a most formidable appearance; the vain allurements with which he was confronted appeared to him serious dangers over which his courage triumphed. The fermented beverage which he imbibed excited his senses and disturbed his reason to the utmost pitch; he murmured his mystic formulas, and they evoked before his distracted imagination divine apparitions. In his ecstasy, he believed himself transported beyond the limits of the world, and having issued from his trance he repeated, as did the mystic of Apuleius:* "I have transcended the boundaries of death, I have trodden the threshold of Proserpine, and having traversed all the elements I am returned to the earth. In the middle of the night I have seen the Sun scintillating with a pure light; I have approached the gods below and the gods above, and have worshipped them face to face."

The tradition of all this occult ceremonial was scrupulously observed by a priesthood instructed in the divine science and distinct from all classes of initiates. Its first founders were certainly the Oriental Magi, but we are almost entirely ignorant of the manner in which its ranks were later recruited and organized. Was it hereditary, named for life, or chosen for a fixed term? In the latter event, who had the

---

*Apuleius, *Metam.* XI, 23, *à propos* of the mystics of Isis.

right of choosing and what conditions did the candidates have to fulfil? None of these points is sufficiently elucidated. We can only state that the priest, who bore indifferently, as it seems, the title of *sacerdos* or that of *antistes*, was often, but not always, a member of the Fathers. We find one vicar, and sometimes several, in each temple. There is every ground for believing that a certain hierarchy existed in this "sacerdotal order." Tertullian tells us that the chief pontiff (*summus ponti-fex*)* could marry but once; he doubtless designated by this Roman name the "Father of the Fathers," who appears to have exercised general jurisdiction over all the initiates residing in the city.† This is the only indication we possess regarding an organization which was perhaps as solidly constituted as that of the Magi in the Sassanian kingdom, or that of the Manichæans of the Roman empire. The same apologist adds that the sectarians of the Persian god also had, like the Christians, their "virgins and their continents." The existence of this kind of Mithraic monachism appears to be all the more remarkable as the merit attached to celibacy is antagonistic to the spirit of Zoroastrianism.

The rôle of the clergy was certainly more extensive than in the ancient Greek and Ro-

---

*Tertull., *De praescr. haeret.*, XL.

†Cf. *supra*, p. 155. I adopt here the suggestion of M. Wissova, *Religion der Römer*, 1902, p. 309.

man religions. The priest was the intermediary between God and man. His functions
evidently included the administration of the
sacraments and the celebration of the services. The inscriptions tell us that in addition
he presided at the formal dedications, or at
least represented the faithful one on such an
occasion along with the Fathers; but this was
the least portion only of the duties he had to
perform; the religious service which fell to
his lot appears to have been very exacting.
He doubtless was compelled to see that a perpetual fire burned upon the altars. Three
times a day, at dawn, at noon, and at dusk, he
addressed a prayer to the Sun, turning in the
morning toward the East, at noon toward the
South, at evening toward the West. The daily
liturgy frequently embraced special sacrifices.
The celebrant, garbed in sacerdotal robes
resembling those of the Magi, sacrificed to the
higher and lower gods divers victims, the blood
of which was collected in a trench; or offered
them libations, holding in his hands the bundle
of sacred twigs which we know from the
Avesta. Long psalmodies and chants accompanied with music were interspersed among
the ritual acts. A solemn moment in the
service,—one very probably marked by the
sounding of a bell,—was that in which the
image of the tauroctonous Mithra, hitherto
kept veiled, was uncovered before the eyes of
the initiates. In some temples, the sculptured

slab, like our tabernacles, revolved on a pivot, and alternately concealed and exposed the figures that adorned its two faces.

Each day in the week, the Planet to which the day was sacred was invoked in a fixed spot in the crypt; and Sunday, over which the Sun presided, was especially holy. Further, the liturgic calendar solemnized certain dates by festivals concerning which we are unfortunately very poorly informed. Possibly the sixteenth or middle day of the month continued (as in Persia) to have Mithra for its patron. On the other hand, there is never a word in the Occident concerning the celebration of the Mithrakana, which were so popular in Asia.* They were doubtless merged in the celebration of the 25th of December, for a very wide-spread custom required that the new birth of the Sun (*Natalis invicti*), which began to wax great again on the termination of the winter solstice, should be celebrated by sacred festivals. We have good reasons for believing that the equinoxes were also days of rejoicing, the return of the deified seasons being inaugurated by some religious salutation. The initiations took place preferably at the beginning of spring, in March or in April, at the Paschal period, when Christians likewise admitted their catechumens to the rites of baptism. But concerning all these solemnities, as generally with everything connected with

*See above, p. 9.

the heortology* of the Mysteries, our ignorance
is almost absolute.

The Mithraic communities were not only
brotherhoods united by spiritual bonds; they
were also associations possessing juridic existence and enjoying the right of holding property.   For the management of their affairs
and the care of their temporal interests, they
elected officers, who must not be confounded
either with the initiates or the priests.   The
titles borne in the descriptions by the members of these boards of trustees prove to us
that the organization of the colleges of the
worshippers of Mithra did not differ from that
of the other religious *sodalicia*, which was
based upon the constitutions of the municipalities or towns.   These corporations published an official list of their members, an
album sacratorum, in which the latter were
ranked according to the importance of their
office.   They had at their head a council of
decurions, a directing committee named most
likely in a general assembly, a sort of minia-
ture senate, of which the first ten (*decem primi*)
possessed, as in the cities, special privileges.
They had their masters (*magistri*) or presi-
dents, elected annually, their curators (*cura-
tores*), upon whom fell the task of manag-
ing the finances, their attorneys (*defensores*),
charged with presenting their cause before

---

*The science of festivals. From ἑορτή, festival, holiday.
—*Tr.*

the courts or public bureaus; and finally, their
patrons (*patroni*), persons of consequence, from
whom they expected not only efficient protection but also pecuniary aid in replenishing
their budget.

As the state granted them no subsidies, their
well-being depended exclusively on private
generosity. Voluntary contributions, the regular revenues of the college, scarcely covered
the expenses of worship, and the least extraordinary expenditure was a heavy burden for
the common purse. These associations of
unmoneyed people could not, with their slen-
der resources, construct sumptuous temples;
ordinarily they acquired from some favorably
disposed land-holder a piece of ground, on
which they erected, or rather dug, their chapel,
some other benefactor defraying the cost of
the construction. Or, some wealthy burgher
placed at the disposal of the mystics a cellar,
where they installed themselves as best they
could. If the original donor had not the
means to pay for the interior decoration of
the crypt and the modelling of the sacred
images, other Brothers supplied the necessary
sum, and a honorific inscription perpetuated
the memory of their munificence. Three
votive inscriptions found in Rome enable us
to witness the founding of one of these Mithraic congregations.*   A freedman and a free-

---

Corpus inscriptionum latinarum, Vol. VI., Nos. 556, 717,
734=30822 (*T. et M.*, Vol. II, p. 101, n°s 47–48bis).

man contributed a marble altar, two other
initiates consecrated a second one, and a slave
likewise made his modest offering. The
generous protectors obtained in return for
their liberality the highest dignities in the
little church. Through their efforts it was
gradually furnished, and in the end could
allow itself certain luxuries. Marble succeeded common stone, sculpture replaced
plaster, and mosaic was substituted for painting. Finally, when the first temple fell into
decay, the enriched community frequently re-
built it with new splendor.

The number of the gifts mentioned in the
epigraphic texts bears witness to the attachment of the faithful to the brotherhoods into
which they had been admitted. It was owing
to the constant devotion of the thousands of
zealous disciples that these societies, the organic cells of the great religious body, could
live and flourish. The order was divided into
a multitude of little circles, strongly knit together and practising the same rites in the
same sanctuaries. The size of the temples in
which they worshipped is proof that the number of members was always very limited.
Even supposing that the Participants only
were allowed to enter the subterranean crypt
and that the initiates of inferior rank were
admitted only to the vestibule (*pronaos*), it is
impossible that these societies should have
counted more than one hundred members.

When the number increased beyond measure, a new chapel was constructed and the group separated. In these compact churches, where every one knew and aided every one else, prevailed the intimacy of a large family. The clear-cut distinctions of an aristocratic society were here effaced; the adoption of the same faith had made the slave the equal, and sometimes the superior, of the decurion and the *clarissimus*. All bowed to the same rules, all were equally honored guests at the same festivals, and after their death they all doubtless reposed in one common sepulcher. Although no Mithraic cemetery has been discovered up to the present day, the special belief of the sect regarding the future life and its very definite rites render it quite probable that like the majority of the Roman *sodalicia* it formed not only religious colleges but also funerary associations. It certainly practised inhumation, and the liveliest and most ardent desire of its adepts must have been that of obtaining an interment that was at once honorable and religious, a "mansion eternal," where they could await in peace the day of the Resurrection. If the name of brothers which the initiates gave themselves was not an empty term, they were bound to render to one another at least this last duty.

The very imperfect image that we can frame of the interior life of the Mithraic conventicles aids us nevertheless in fathoming the reasons of their rapid multiplication. The humble plebeians who first entered its vaults in great numbers found in the fraternity of these congregations succor and solace. In joining them, they passed from their isolation and abandonment to become a part of a powerful organization with a fully developed hierarchy and having ramifications that spread like a dense net over the entire empire. Besides, the titles which were conferred upon them satisfied the natural desire that dwells in every man of playing a part in the world and of enjoying some consideration in the eyes of his fellows.

With these purely secular reasons were associated the more powerful motives of faith. The members of these little societies imagined themselves in the privileged possession of a body of ancient wisdom derived from the far Orient. The secrecy with which these unfathomable arcana were surrounded increased the veneration that they inspired: *Omne ignotum pro magnifico est*. The gradual initiations kept alive in the heart of the neophyte the hopes of truth still more sublime, and the strange rites which accompanied them left in his ingenuous soul an ineffaceable impression. The converts believed they found, and, the suggestion being transformed into reality, actually did find, in the mystic ceremonies a stimulant and a consolation. They believed themselves purified of their guilt by the ritual ablutions, and this baptism lightened their conscience of the weight of their heavy responsibility. They came forth strengthened from these sacred banquets, which contained the promise of a better life, where the sufferings of this world would find their full compensation. The astonishing spread of Mithraism is due in large measure to these stupendous illusions, which would appear ludicrous were they not so profoundly and thoroughly human.

Nevertheless, in the competition between the rival churches that disputed under the Cæsars the empire of human souls, one cause of inferiority rendered the struggle unequal for the Persian sect. Whilst the majority of the Oriental cults accorded to women a considerable rôle in their churches, and sometimes even a preponderating one, finding in them ardent supporters of the faith, Mithra forbade their participation in his Mysteries and so deprived himself of the incalculable assistance of these propagandists. The rude discipline of the order did not permit them to take the degrees in the sacred cohorts, and, as among the Mazdeans of the Orient, they occupied only a secondary place in the society of the faithful. Among the hundreds of inscriptions that have come down to us, not one mentions either a priestess, a woman initiate, or even a donatress. But a religion which aspired to become universal could not deny a knowledge of divine things to one half of the human race, and in order to afford some opportunity for feminine devotion it contracted at Rome an alliance which certainly contributed to its success. The history of Mithraism in the Occident would not be intelligible if we neglected to consider its policy toward the rest of paganism.

MITHRAISM AND THE RELIGIONS OF
THE EMPIRE

THE acts of the Oriental martyrs bear eloquent testimony to the intolerance of the national clergy of the Persia of the Sassanids; and the Magi of the ancient empire, if they were not persecutors, at least constituted an exclusive caste, and possibly even a privileged race. The priests of Mithra afford no evidence of having assumed a like attitude. Like the Judaism of Alexandria, Mazdaism had been softened in Asia Minor by the Hellenic civilization. Transported into a strange world, it was compelled to accommodate itself to the usages and ideas there prevailing; and the favor with which it was received encouraged it to persevere in its policy of conciliation. The Iranian gods who accompanied Mithra in his peregrinations were worshipped in the Occident under Greek and Latin names; the Avestan *yazatas* assumed there the guise of the immortals enthroned on Olympus, and these facts are in themselves sufficient to prove that far from exhibiting hostility toward the ancient Græco-Roman beliefs, the Asiatic religion sought to accommodate itself to them, in appearance at least. A pious mystic could, without renoun-

cing his faith, dedicate a votive inscription to
the Capitoline triad,—Jupiter, Juno, and Minerva; he merely invested these divine names

Fig. 40.

TAUROCTONOUS MITHRA

In the possession of Mr. S. H. Janes, Janes Buildings, Toronto, Canada. With the usual accessories. In
the upper left-hand corner a bust of the Sun, and in
the upper right-hand corner a bust of the Moon. The
left hand of the god, which has been broken off, apparently grasps a horn and not the nostrils of the bull.
In all probability partly restored, it being scarcely
possible that the dadophori could both have held
upright torches. (*T. et M.*, Fig. 418, p. 483.)

with a different meaning from their ordinary
acceptation. If the injunction to refrain from
participating in other Mysteries, which is said
to have been imposed upon Mithraic initiates,

was ever obeyed it was not long able to withstand the syncretic tendencies of imperial paganism. For in the fourth century the "Fathers of the Fathers" were found performing the highest offices of the priesthood, in temples of all sorts.

Everywhere the sect knew how to adapt itself with consummate skill to the environment in which it lived. In the valley of the Danube it exercised on the indigenous cult an influence that presupposes a prolonged contact between them. In the region of the Rhine, the Celtic divinities were worshipped in the crypts of the Persian god, or at least alongside of them. Thus, the Mazdean theology, according to the country in which it flourished, was colored with variable tints, the precise gradations of which it is now impossible for us to follow. But these dogmatic shadings merely diversified the subordinate details of the religion, and never imperilled its fundamental unity. There is not the slightest evidence that these deviations of a flexible doctrine provoked heresies. The concessions which it made were matters of pure form. In reality, Mithraism having arrived in the Occident in its full maturity, and even showing signs of decrepitude, no longer assimilated the elements that it borrowed from the surrounding life. The only influences that profoundly modified its character were those to which it was subjected in its youth amidst the populations of Asia.

The close relation in which Mithra stood to certain gods of this country is explained not only by the natural affinity which united all Oriental immigrants in opposition to the paganism of Greece and Rome. The ancient religious hostility of the Egyptians and Persians persisted even in Rome under the emperors, and the Iranian Mysteries appear to have been separated from those of Isis by secret rivalry if not by open opposition. On the other hand, they associated readily with the Syrian cults that had emigrated with them from Asia and Europe. Their doctrines, thoroughly imbued with Chaldæan theories, must have presented a striking resemblance to that of the Semitic religions. Jupiter Dolichenus, who was worshipped simultaneously with Mithra in Commagene, the land of his origin, and who like the latter remained a preëminently military divinity, is found by his side in all the countries of the Occident. At Carnuntum in Pannonia, a mithræum and a *dolichenum** adjoined each other. Baal, the lord of the heavens, was readily identified with Ormazd, who had become Jupiter-Cælus, and Mithra was easily likened to the solar god of the Syrians. Even the rites of the two liturgies appear to have offered some resemblances.

As in Commagene, so also in Phrygia, Mazdaism had sought a common ground of understanding with the religion of the country. In

---

*A temple of Jupiter Dolichenus.—*Tr.*

the union of Mithra and Anâhita the counterpart was found of the intimacy between the
great indigenous divinities Attis and Cybele,
and this harmony between the two sacred
couples persisted in Italy. The most ancient
mithræum known to us was contiguous to the
*metroon** of Ostia, and we have every reason
to believe that the worship of the Iranian god
and that of the Phrygian goddess were conducted in intimate communion with each other
throughout the entire extent of the empire.
Despite the profound differences of their character, political reasons drew them together.
In conciliating the priests of the *Mater Magna*,
the sectaries of Mithra obtained the support
of a powerful and officially recognized clergy,
and so shared in some measure in the protection afforded it by the State. Further, since
men only were permitted to take part in the
secret ceremonies of the Persian liturgy, other
Mysteries to which women were admitted must
have formed some species of alliance with the
former, to make them complete. The Great
Mother succeeded thus to the place of Anâhita; she had her *Matres* or "Mothers," as
Mithra had his "Fathers"; and her initiates
were known among one another as "Sisters,"
just as the votaries of her associate called
one another "Brothers."

This alliance, fruitful generally in its results,
was especially profitable to the ancient cult of

_____

* A temple of Cybele. — *Tr.*

Pessinus, now naturalized at Rome. The loud pomp of its festivals was a poor mask of the vacuity of its doctrines, which no longer satisfied the aspirations of its devotees. Its gross theology was elevated by the adoption of certain Mazdean beliefs. There can be scarcely any doubt that the practice of the taurobolium, with the ideas of purification and immortality appertaining to it, had passed under the Antonines from the temples of Anâhita into those of the *Mater Magna*. The barbarous custom of allowing the blood of a victim slaughtered on a latticed platform to fall down upon the mystic lying in a pit below, was probably practised in Asia from time immemorial. According to a wide-spread notion among primitive peoples, the blood is the vehicle of the vital energy, and the person who poured it upon his body and moistened his tongue with it, believed that he was thereby endowed with the courage and strength of the slaughtered animal. This sacred bath appears to have been administered in Cappadocia in a great number of sanctuaries, and especially in those of Mâ, the great indigenous divinity, and in those of Anâhita. These goddesses, to whom the bull was consecrated, had been generally likened by the Greeks to their Artemis Tauropolos, and the ritualistic baptism practised in their cult received the name of *tauropolium* (ταυροπόλιον), which was transformed by the popular etymology into *tauro-*

bolium (ταυροβόλιον). But under the influence of the Mazdean beliefs regarding the future life, a more profound significance was attributed to this baptism of blood. In taking it the devotees no longer imagined they acquired the strength of the bull; it was no longer a renewal of physical strength that the life-sustaining liquid was now thought to communicate, but a renovation, temporary or even perpetual, of the human soul.*

When, under the empire, the taurobolium was introduced into Italy, it was not quite certain at the outset what Latin name should be given the goddess in whose honor it was celebrated. Some saw in her a celestial Venus; others compared her to Minerva, because of her warlike character. But the priests of Cybele soon introduced the ceremony into their liturgy,—evidently with the complicity of the official authorities, for nothing in the ritual of this recognized cult could be modified without the authorization of the quindecemvirs. Even the emperors are known to have granted privileges to those who performed this hideous sacrifice for their salvation, though their motives for this special favor are not clearly apparent. The efficacy which was attributed to this bloody purification, the eternal new birth that was expected of it, resem-

---

*These pages summarize the conclusions of a study entitled *Le taurobole et le culte de Bellone*, published in the *Revue d'histoire et de littérature religieuses*.

bled the hopes which the mystics of Mithra attached to the immolation of the mythical bull.* The similarity of these doctrines is quite naturally explained by the identity of their origin. The taurobolium, like many rites of the Oriental cults, is a survival of a savage past which a spiritualistic theology had adapted to moral ends. It is a characteristic fact that the first immolations of this kind that we know to have been performed by the clergy of the Phrygian goddess took place at Ostia, where the *metroon*, as we saw above, adjoined a Mithraic crypt.

The symbolism of the Mysteries certainly saw in the *Magna Mater* the nourishing Earth which the Heavens yearly fecundated. So the Græco-Roman divinities which they adopted changed in character on entering their dogmatic system. Sometimes, these gods were identified with the Mazdean heroes, and the barbaric legends then celebrated the new exploits which they had performed. Sometimes, they were considered the agents that produced the various transformations of the universe. Then, in the center of this pantheon, which had again become naturalistic, as it was at its origin, was placed the Sun, for he was the supreme lord that governed the movements of all the planets and even the revolutions of the heavens themselves,—the one who suffused with his light and his heat

* See above, p. 146.

all of life here below. This conception, astronomical in its origin, predominated more and more according as Mithra entered into more intimate relations with Greek thought

Mithra slaying the bull. On the reverse Cupid
and Psyche (broken).

Obverse: The sun-god standing upright on his quadriga and holding in his hand the globe on which the four quarters are indicated. Reverse: Mithra leading off the bull. (Metropolitan Museum of Art, New York.)

Fig. 41.

MITHRAIC GEMS.

Green jasper. (*T. et M.*, p. 449.)

and became a more faithful subject of the Roman state.

The worship of the Sun, the outcome of a sentiment of recognition for its daily benefactions, augmented by the observation of its tremendous rôle in the cosmic system, was the logical upshot of paganism. When critical thought sought to explain the sacred traditions and discovered in the popular gods the forces and elements of nature, it was obliged perforce to accord a predominant place to the star on which the very existence of our globe depended. "Before religion reached the point where it proclaimed that God should be sought in the Absolute and the Ideal, that is to say, outside the world, one cult only was reasonable and scientific and that was the cult of the Sun."* From the time of Plato and Aristotle, Greek philosophy regarded the celestial bodies as animate and divine creatures; Stoicism furnished new arguments in favor of this opinion; while Neo-Pythagorism and Neo-Platonism insisted still more emphatically on the sacred character of the luminary which is the ever-present image of the intelligible God. These beliefs, approved by the thinkers, were widely diffused by literature, and particularly by the works in which romantic fiction served to envelop genuinely theological teachings.

If heliolatry was in accord with the philosophical doctrines of the day, it was not less in conformity with its political tendencies. We have essayed to show the connection which existed between the worship of the emperors

* Renan, *Lettre à Berthelot* (*Dialogues et fragments philosophiques*), p. 168.

and that of the *Sol invictus*. When the Cæsars
of the third century pretended to be gods descended from heaven to the earth, the justification of their imaginary claims had as its corollary the establishment of a public worship of the
divinity from whom they believed themselves
the emanations. Heliogabalus had claimed
for his Baal of Emesa the supremacy over the

Fig. 42.

MITHRAIC CAMEO (RED JASPER).

Principal face: In the center, the tauroctonous
Mithra, with the dog, the scorpion, the two torch-
bearers, etc. Reverse: A lion with a bee in his
mouth; above, seven stars surrounded by magic
Greek inscriptions. (*T. et M.*, p. 450.)

entire pagan pantheon. The eccentricities
and violences of this unbalanced man resulted
in the lamentable wreck of his undertaking;
but it answered to the needs of the time and
was soon taken up again with better success.
Near the Flaminian Way, to the east of the
Field of Mars, Aurelian consecrated a colossal
edifice to the tutelary god that had granted
him victory in Syria. The religion of state

that he constituted must not be confounded
with Mithraism. Its imposing temple, its
ostentatious ceremonies, its quadrennial
games, its pontifical clergy, remind us of the
great sanctuaries of the Orient and not of the
dim caves in which the Mysteries were cele-

Fig. 43.

SOL THE SUN-GOD.

Installed by Mithra as the governor of the world. To the
right the globe of power. (*T. et M.*, p. 202.)

brated. Nevertheless, the *Sol invictus*, whom
the emperor had intended to honor with a
pomp hitherto unheard of, could well be
claimed as their own by the followers of
Mithra.

The imperial policy gave the first place in
the official religion to the Sun, of which the
sovereign was the emanation, just as in the

Chaldæan speculations propagated by the Mithraists the royal planet held sway over the other stars. On both sides, the growing tendency was to see in the brilliant star that illuminated the universe the only God, or at least the sensible image of the only God, and to establish in the heavens a monotheism in imitation of the monarchy that ruled on earth. Macrobius (400 A.D.), in his *Saturnalia*, has learnedly set forth that the gods were ultimately reducible to a single Being considered under different aspects, and that the multiple names by which they were worshipped were the equivalent of that of Helios (the Sun). The theologian Vettius Agorius Prætextatus who defended this radical syncrasy was not only one of the highest dignitaries of the empire, but one of the last chiefs of the Persian Mysteries.

Mithraism, at least in the fourth century, had therefore as its end and aim the union of all gods and all myths in a vast synthesis,—the foundation of a new religion in harmony with the prevailing philosophy and political constitution of the empire. This religion would have been as far removed from the ancient Iranian Mazdaism as from Græco-Roman paganism, which accorded the sidereal powers a minimal place only. It had in a measure traced idolatry back to its origin, and discovered in the myths that obscured its comprehension the deification of nature.

Breaking with the Roman principle of the na-
tionality of worship, it would have established
the universal domination of Mithra, identified
with the invincible Sun. Its adherents hoped,
by concentrating all their devotion upon a
single object, to impart new cohesion to the
disintegrated beliefs. Solar pantheism was
the last refuge of conservative spirits, now
menaced by a revolutionary propaganda that
aimed at the annihilation of the entire ancient
order of things.

At the time when this pagan monotheism
sought to establish its ascendency in Rome,
the struggle between the Mithraic Mysteries
and Christianity had long begun. The propagation of the two religions had been almost
contemporaneously conducted, and their diffusion had taken place under analogous conditions. Both from the Orient, they had spread
because of the same general reasons, viz., the
political unity and the moral anarchy of the
empire. Their diffusion had been accomplished with like rapidity, and toward the close
of the second century they both numbered
adherents in the most distant parts of the
Roman world. The sectaries of Mithra might
justly lay claim to the hyperbolic utterance of
Tertullian: "*Hesterni sumus et vestra omnia im-
plevimus.*" If we consider the number of the
monuments that the Persian religion has left
us, one may easily ask whether in the epoch
of the Severi its adepts were not more numer-

ous than the disciples of Christ. Another
point of resemblance between the two antagonistic creeds was that at the outset they drew
their proselytes chiefly from the inferior
classes of society; their propaganda was at
the origin essentially popular; unlike the philosophical sects, they addressed their endeav-
ors less to cultivated minds than to the masses,
and consequently appealed more to sentiment
than to reason.

But by the side of these resemblances considerable differences are to be remarked in
the methods of procedure of the two adversaries. The initial conquests of Christianity
were favored by the Jewish diaspora, and it
first spread in the countries inhabited by
Israelitic colonies. It was therefore chiefly in
the countries washed by the Mediterranean
that its communities developed. They did
not extend their field of action outside the
cities, and their multiplication is due in great
part to missions undertaken with the express
purpose of "instructing the nations." The extension of Mithraism, on the other hand, was
essentially a natural product of social and
political factors; namely, of the importation
of slaves, the transportation of troops, and
the transfer of public functionaries. It was in
government circles and in the army that it
counted its greatest number of votaries,—that
is, in circles where very few Christians could
be found because of their aversion to official

paganism. Outside of Italy, it spread principally along the frontiers and simultaneously gained a foothold in the cities and in the country. It found its strongest points of support in the Danubian provinces and in Germany, whereas Christianity made most rapid progress in Asia Minor and Syria. The spheres of the two religious powers, therefore, were not coincident, and they could accordingly long grow and develop without coming directly into conflict. It was in the valley of the Rhone, in Africa, and especially in the city of Rome, where the two competitors were most firmly established, that the rivalry, during the third century, became particularly brisk between the bands of Mithra's worshippers and the disciples of Christ.

The struggle between the two rival religions was the more stubborn as their characters were the more alike. The adepts of both formed secret conventicles, closely united, the members of which gave themselves the name of "Brothers."* The rites which they practised offered numerous analogies. The sectaries of the Persian god, like the Christians, purified themselves by baptism; received, by a species of confirmation, the power necessary to combat the spirits of evil; and expected

---

* I may remark that even the expression "dearest brothers" had already been used by the sectaries of Jupiter Dolichenus (CIL, VI, 406=30758: *fratres carissimos et conlegas hon [estissimos]*) and probably also in the Mithraic associations.

from a Lord's Supper salvation of body and soul. Like the latter, they also held Sunday sacred, and celebrated the birth of the Sun on the 25th of December, the same day on which Christmas has been celebrated, since the fourth century at least. They both preached a categorical system of ethics, regarded asceticism as meritorious, and counted among their principal virtues abstinence and continence, renunciation and self-control. Their conceptions of the world and of the destiny of man were similar. They both admitted the existence of a Heaven inhabited by beatified ones, situate in the upper regions, and of a Hell peopled by demons, situate in the bowels of the earth. They both placed a Flood at the beginning of history; they both assigned as the source of their traditions a primitive revelation; they both, finally, believed in the immortality of the soul, in a last judgment, and in a resurrection of the dead, consequent upon a final conflagration of the universe.

We have seen that the theology of the Mysteries made of Mithra a "mediator" equivalent to the Alexandrian Logos. Like him, Christ also was a μεσίτης, an intermediary between his celestial father and men, and like him he also was one of a trinity. These resemblances were certainly not the only ones that pagan exegesis established between the two religions, and the figure of the tauroctonous god reluctantly immolating his victim that he might

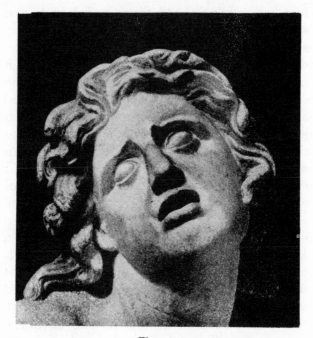

Fig. 44.

THE PASSION OF THE GOD.

The Dying Alexander, so called. Type of a group of sculptures from the school of Pergamon, dating from the second century before Christ. The idealized portrait of Alexander as solar god has been discovered in the head of the celebrated Mithraic statue of the Capitol (see Fig. 4, page 21), and the facial expressions of dolor, pathos, and compassion which characterize this work are shared by all the more important representations of the Mithraic sacrifice. The present sculpture has been partly restored, and it is therefore impossible to determine absolutely whether it originally formed part of an Asiatic group of the tauroctonous Mithra. (*T. et M., Introduction*, p. 182.)

create and save the human race, was certainly compared to the picture of the redeemer sacrificing his own person for the salvation of the world.

On the other hand, the ecclesiastical writers, reviving a metaphor of the prophet Malachi, contrasted the "Sun of justice" with the "invincible Sun," and consented to see in the dazzling orb which illuminated men a symbol of Christ, "the light of the world." Should we be astonished if the multitudes of devotees failed always to observe the subtle distinctions of the doctors, and if in obedience to a pagan custom they rendered to the radiant star of day the homage which orthodoxy reserved for God? In the fifth century, not only heretics, but even faithful followers, were still wont to bow their heads toward its dazzling disc as it rose above the horizon, and to murmur the prayer, "Have mercy upon us."

The resemblances between the two hostile churches were so striking as to impress even the minds of antiquity. From the third century, the Greek philosophers were wont to draw parallels between the Persian Mysteries and Christianity which were evidently entirely in favor of the former. The Apologists also dwelt on the analogies between the two religions, and explained them as a Satanic travesty of the holiest rites of their religion. If the polemical works of the Mithraists had been preserved, we should doubtless have heard the same accusation hurled back upon their Christian adversaries.

We cannot presume to unravel to-day a question which divided contemporaries and which shall doubtless forever remain insoluble. We are too imperfectly acquainted with the dogmas and liturgies of Roman Mazdaism, as well as with the development of primitive Christianity, to say definitely what mutual influences were operative in their simultaneous evolution. But be this as it may, resemblances do not necessarily suppose an imitation. Many correspondences between the Mithraic doctrine and the Catholic faith are explicable by their common Oriental origin. Nevertheless, certain ideas and certain ceremonies must necessarily have passed from the one cult to the other; but in the majority of cases we rather suspect this transference than clearly perceive it.

Apparently the attempt was made to discern in the legend of the Iranian hero the counterpart of the life of Jesus, and the disciples of the Magi probably drew a direct contrast between the Mithraic worship of the shepherds, the Mithraic communion and ascension, and those of the Gospels. The rock of generation, which had given birth to the genius of light, was even compared to the immovable rock, emblem of Christ, upon which the Church was founded; and the crypt in which the bull had perished was made the counterpart of that in which Christ is said to have been born at Bethlehem.* But this strained parallelism could result in nothing but a caricature. It was a strong source of inferiority for Mazdaism that it believed in only a mythical redeemer. That unfailing wellspring of religious emotion supplied by the teachings and the passion of the God sacrificed on the cross, never flowed for the disciples of Mithra.

On the other hand, the orthodox and heretical liturgies of Christianity, which gradually sprang up during the first centuries of our era, could find abundant inspiration in the Mithraic Mysteries, which of all the pagan religions offered the most affinity with Christian institutions. We do not know whether the ritual of the sacraments and the hopes attaching to them suffered alteration through the influence of Mazdean dogmas and practices. Perhaps the custom of invoking the Sun three times each day,—at dawn, at noon, and at dusk,—was

---

* M. Jean Réville (*Études publiées en hommage à la faculté de théologie de Montauban*, 1901, pp. 339 *et seq.*) thinks that the Gospel story of the birth of Christ and the adoration of the Magi was suggested by the Mithraic legend; but he remarks that we have no proof of the supposition. So also M. A. Dieterich in a recent article (*Zeitschr. f. Neutest. Wiss.*, 1902, p. 190), in which he has endeavored not without ingenuity to explain the formation of the legend of the Magi kings, admits that the worship of the shepherds was introduced into Christian tradition from Mazdaism. But I must remark that the Mazdean beliefs regarding the advent of Mithra into the world have strangely varied. (*Cf. T. et M.*, Vol. I., pp. 160 *et seq.*)

reproduced in the daily prayers of the Church, and it appears certain that the commemoration of the Nativity was set for the 25th of December, because it was at the winter solstice that the rebirth of the invincible god,* the *Natalis invicti,* was celebrated. In adopting this date, which was universally distinguished by sacred festivities, the ecclesiastical

Fig. 45.

BAS-RELIEF OF MAYENCE.

Mithra drawing his bow; and the god of the winds.

authority purified in some measure the profane usages which it could not suppress.

The only domain in which we can ascertain in detail the extent to which Christianity imitated Mithraism is that of art. The Mithraic sculpture, which had been first developed, furnished the ancient Christian marble-cutters with a large number of models, which they adopted or adapted. For example, they drew

* See above, p. 167.

inspiration from the figure of Mithra causing the living waters to leap forth by the blows of his arrows,* to create the figure of Moses smiting with his rod the rock of Horeb (Fig. 45). Faithful to an inveterate tradition, they even reproduced the figures of cosmic divinities, like the Heavens and the Winds, the worship of which the new faith had expressly proscribed; and we find on the sarcophagi, in miniatures, and even on the portals of the Romance Churches, evidences of the influence exerted by the imposing compositions that adorned the sacred grottos of Mithra.†

It would be wrong, however, to exaggerate the significance of these likenesses. If Christianity and Mithraism offered profound resemblances, the principal of which were the belief in the purification of souls and the hope of a beatific resurrection, differences no less essential separated them. The most important was the contrast of their relations to Roman paganism. The Mazdean Mysteries sought to conciliate paganism by a succession of adaptations and compromises; they endeavored to establish monotheism while not combating polytheism, whereas the Church was, in point of principle, if not always in practice, the unrelenting antagonist of idolatry in any form. The attitude of Mithraism was apparently the wiser; it gave to the Persian relig-

* See above, p. 138.
† See p. 227.

ion greater elasticity and powers of adaptation, and it attracted toward the tauroctonous god all who stood in dread of a painful rupture with ancient traditions and contemporaneous society. The preference must therefore have been given by many to dogmas that satisfied their aspirations for greater purity and a better world, without compelling them to detest the faith of their fathers and the State of which they were citizens. As the Church grew in power despite its persecutors, this policy of compromise first assured to Mithraism much tolerance and afterward even the favor of the public authorities. But it also prevented it from freeing itself of the gross and ridiculous superstitions which complicated its ritual and its theology; it involved it, in spite of its austerity, in an equivocal alliance with the orgiastic cult of the beloved of Attis; and it compelled it to carry the entire weight of a chimerical and odious past. If Romanized Mazdaism had triumphed, it would not only have preserved from oblivion all the aberrations of pagan mysticism, but would also have perpetuated the erroneous doctrine of physics on which its dogmatism reposed. The Christian doctrine, which broke with the cults of nature, remained exempt from these impure associations, and its liberation from every compromising attachment assured it an immense superiority. Its negative value, its struggle against deeply-rooted prejudices, gained for it as many souls as did the positive hopes which it promised. It performed the miraculous feat of triumphing over the ancient world in spite of legislation and the imperial policy, and the Mithraic Mysteries were promptly abolished the moment the protection of the State was withdrawn and transformed into hostility.

Mithraism reached the apogee of its power toward the middle of the third century, and it appeared for a moment as if the world was on the verge of becoming Mithraic. But the first invasions of the barbarians, and especially the definitive loss of Dacia (275 A.D.), soon after followed by that of the Agri Decumates, administered a terrible blow to the Mazdean sect, which was most powerful in the periphery of the *orbis Romanus*. In all Pannonia, and as far as Virunum, on the frontiers of Italy, its temples were sacked. By way of compensation, the authorities, menaced by the rapid progress of Christianity, renewed their support to the most redoubtable adversary that they could oppose to it. In the universal downfall the army was the only institution that remained standing, and the Cæsars created by the legions were bound perforce to seek their support in the favored religion of their soldiers. In 273 A.D., Aurelian founded by the side of the Mysteries of the tauroctonous god a public religion, which he richly endowed, in honor of the *Sol invictus*. Dio-

cletian, whose court with its complicated hierarchy, its prostrations before its lord, and its
crowds of eunuchs, was, by the admission of
contemporaries, an imitation of the court of
the Sassanids, was naturally inclined to adopt
doctrines of Persian origin, which flattered his
despotic instincts. The emperor and the
princes whom he had associated with himself,
meeting in conference at Carnuntum in 307
A.D., restored there one of the temples of the
celestial protector of their newly-organized
empire.* The Christians believed, not without some appearance of reason, that the Mithraic clergy were the instigators of the great
persecutions under Galerius. In the Roman
empire as in Iran, a vaguely monistic heliolatry appeared on the verge of becoming the
sole, intolerant religion of state. But the conversion of Constantine shattered the hopes
which the policy of his predecessors had held
out to the worshippers of the sun. Although
he did not persecute the beliefs which he himself had shared,† they ceased to constitute a
recognized cult and were tolerated only. His
successors were outspokenly hostile. To
latent defiance succeeded open persecution.
Christian polemics no longer restricted its
attacks to ridiculing the legends and practices
of the Mazdean Mysteries, nor even to taunt-

---

* See above, pp. 88-89.
†*Cf.* Preger, *Konstantinos-Helios* (Hermes, XXXVI), 1901,
p. 457.

ing them for having as their founders the irreconcilable enemies of Rome; it now stridently demanded the total destruction of idolatry, and its exhortations were promptly carried into effect. When a rhetorician* tells us that under Constantius no one longer dared to look at the rising or setting sun, that even farmers and sailors refrained from observing the stars, and tremblingly held their eyes fixed upon the ground, we have in these emphatic declarations a magnified echo of the fears that then filled all pagan hearts.

The proclamation of Julian the Apostate (331–363 A.D.) suddenly inaugurated an unexpected turn in affairs. A philosopher, seated on the throne by the armies of Gaul, Julian had cherished from childhood a secret devotion for Helios. He was firmly convinced that this god had rescued him from the perils that menaced his youth; he believed that he was entrusted by him with a divine mission, and regarded himself as his servitor, or rather as his spiritual son. He dedicated to this celestial "king" a discourse in which the ardor of his faith transforms in places a cold theological dissertation into an inflamed dithyrambic, and the fervor of his devotion for the star that he worshipped never waned to the moment of his death.

The young prince had been presumably drawn to the Mysteries by his superstitious

---

* Mamert., *Grat. actio in Iulian.*, c. 23.

predilection for the supernatural. Before his
accession, perhaps even from youth, he had
been introduced secretly into a Mithraic con-
venticle by the philosopher Maximus of Eph-
esus. The ceremonies of his initiation must
have made a deep impression on his feelings.
He imagined himself thenceforward under the
special patronage of Mithra, in this life and in
that to come. As soon as he had cast aside
his mask and openly proclaimed himself a
pagan, he called Maximus to his side, and
doubtless had recourse to extraordinary ablutions and purifications to wipe out the stains
which he had contracted in receiving the baptism and the communion of the Christians.
Scarcely had he ascended the throne (361 A.D.)
than he made haste to introduce the Persian cult
at Constantinople; and almost simultaneously
the first taurobolia were celebrated at Athens.

On all sides the sectaries of the Magi lifted
their heads. At Alexandria the patriarch
George, in attempting to erect a church on the
ruins of a mithræum, provoked a sanguinary
riot. Arrested by the magistrates, he was
torn from his prison and cruelly slain by the
populace on the 24th of December, 361, the
eve of the *Natalis invicti*. The emperor contented himself with addressing a paternal
remonstrance to the city of Serapis.

But the Apostate soon met his death in the
historic expedition against the Persians, to
which he had possibly been drawn by the

secret desire to conquer the land which had given him his faith and by the assurance that his tutelary god would accept his homage rather than that of his enemies. Thus perished this spasmodic attempt at reaction, and Christianity, now definitively victor, addressed itself to the task of extirpating the erroneous doctrine that had caused it so much anxiety. Even before the emperors had forbidden the exercise of idolatry, their edicts against astrology and magic furnished an indirect means of attacking the clergy and disciples of Mithra. In 371 A.D., a number of persons who cultivated occult practices were implicated in a pretended conspiracy and put to death. The mystagogue Maximus himself perished as the victim of an accusation of this kind.

It was not long before the imperial government legislated formally and directly against the disgraced sect. In the provinces, popular uprisings frequently anticipated the interference of the magistrates. Mobs sacked the temples and committed them to the flames, with the complicity of the authorities. The ruins of the mithræums bear witness to the violence of their devastating fury. Even at Rome, in 377 A.D., the prefect Gracchus, seeking the privilege of baptism, offered as a pledge of the sincerity of his conversion the "destruction, shattering, and shivering,"* of a

---

* St. Jerome, *Epist. 107 ad Lætam* (*T. et M.*, Vol. II., p. 18), *subvertit, fregit, excussit.*

Mithraic crypt, with all the statues that it contained. Frequently, in order to protect their grottoes from pillage by making them inaccessible, the priests walled up the entrances, or conveyed their sacred images to well-protected hiding-places, convinced that the tem-

Fig. 46.

CHAINED SKELETON.

Discovered in the ruins of a Mithraic temple at Sarrebourg, in Lorraine. (*T. et M.*, p. 519.)

pest that had burst upon them was momentary only, and that after their days of trial their god would cause again to shine forth the light of final triumph. On the other hand, the Christians, in order to render places contaminated by the presence of a dead body ever afterward unfit for worship, sometimes slew the refractory priests of Mithra and buried them in the ruins of their sanctuaries, now forever profaned (Fig. 46).

The hope of restoration was especially tenacious at Rome, which remained the capital of paganism. The aristocracy, still faithful to the traditions of their ancestors, supported the religion with their wealth and prestige. Its members loved to deck themselves with the titles of "Father and Herald of Mithra Invincible," and multiplied the offerings and the foundations. They redoubled their generosity toward him when Gratian in 382 A.D. despoiled their temples of their wealth. A great lord recounts to us in poor verses how he had restored a splendid crypt erected by his grandfather near the Flaminian Way, boasting that he was able to dispense with public subsidies of any kind.* The usurpation of Eugenius appeared for a moment to bring on the expected resurrection. The prefect of the prætorium, Nicomachus Flavianus, celebrated solemn taurobolia and renewed in a sacred cave the Mysteries of the "associate god" (*deum comitem*) of the pretender. But the victory of Theodosius, 394 A.D., shattered once and for all the hopes of these belated partisans of the ancient Mazdean belief.

A few clandestine conventicles may, with stubborn persistence, have been held in the

---

*CIL, VI, (*T. et M.*, Vol. II, p. 94, No. 13).

subterranean retreats of the palaces. The cult of the Persian god possibly existed as late as the fifth century in certain remote cantons of the Alps and the Vosges. For example, devotion to the Mithraic rites long persisted in the tribe of the Anauni, masters of a flourishing valley, of which a narrow defile closed the mouth. But little by little its last disciples in the Latin countries abandoned a religion tainted with moral as well as political decadence. It maintained its ground with greater tenacity in the Orient, the land of its birth. Driven out of the rest of the empire, it found a refuge in the countries of its origin, where its light only slowly flickered out.

Nevertheless, the conceptions which Mithraism had diffused throughout the empire during a period of three centuries were not destined to perish with it. Some of them, even those most characteristic of it, such as its ideas concerning Hell, the efficacy of the sacraments, and the resurrection of the flesh, were accepted even by its adversaries; and in disseminating them it had simply accelerated their universal domination. Certain of its sacred practices continued to exist also in the ritual of Christian festivals and in popular usage. Its fundamental dogmas, however, were irreconcilable with orthodox Christianity, outside of which only they could maintain their hold. Its theory of sidereal influences, alternately condemned and tolerated, was carried down by astrology to the threshold of modern times; but it was to a religion more powerful than this false science that the Persian Mysteries were destined to bequeath, along with their hatred of the Church, their cardinal ideas and their influence over the masses.

Manichæism, although the work of a man and not the product of a long evolution, was connected with these Mysteries by numerous affinities. The tradition according to which its original founders had conversed in Persia with the priests of Mithra may be inexact in form, but it involves nevertheless a profound truth. Both religions had been formed in the Orient from a mixture of the ancient Babylonian mythology with Persian dualism, and had afterward absorbed Hellenic elements. The sect of Manichæus spread throughout the empire during the fourth century, at the moment when Mithraism was expiring, and it was called to assume the latter's succession. Mystics whom the polemics of the Church against paganism had shaken but not converted were enraptured with the new conciliatory faith which suffered Zoroaster and Christ to be simultaneously worshipped. The wide diffusion which the Mazdean beliefs with their mixture of Chaldæism had enjoyed, prepared the minds of the empire for the reception of the new heresy. The latter found its way made smooth for it, and this is the secret of

its sudden expansion. Thus renewed, the
Mithraic doctrines were destined to withstand
for centuries all persecutions, and rising again
in a new form in the Middle Ages to shake
once more the ancient Roman world.

MITHRAIC ART *

THE monuments of Mithraism, which have been found in considerable numbers in the provinces of the Occident and even in the Orient, constitute a homogeneous group, of which it is desirable to characterize the importance for the history of Roman art. In point of fact, their artistic merit is far below that of their value as historical documents, and their chief worth is not æsthetic but religious. The late epoch in which these works were produced destroys the least hope of finding in them any expression of true creative power or of following in them the progress of any original development. But it would be unjust if, inspired by a narrow-minded Atticism, we should cast upon them all a like measure of reproach. In the absence of inventive genius, their cleverness in the adaptation of ancient *motifs* and the manual skill shown in their execution,—all technical qualities of which they give evidence,—would alone be sufficient to claim our attention. Some of the groups in high and low relief,—for the paintings and mosaics which have been preserved are so few and mediocre as to dispense us from speaking

---

*In the original this chapter appeared as an Appendix. We have given it an independent place in this edition.—*Tr*.

of them,—hold a very honorable place in the multitude of sculptured works which the imperial period has left us, and are deserving of some consideration.

It can be proved* that all our representations of the tauroctonous Mithra, the hieratic figure of which was fixed before the propagation of the Mysteries in the Occident, are more or less faithful replicas of a type created by a sculptor of the school of Pergamon, in imitation of the sacrificing Victory which adorned the balustrade of the temple of Athena Nike on the Acropolis. Certain marbles discovered at Rome and at Ostia (see for example, Figs. 4, 5, 6 and 10), which unquestionably go back to the beginning of the second century, still reflect the splendor of the powerful compositions of the Hellenistic epoch. After an ardent pursuit, the god captures the bull, which has fallen to the earth; with one knee on its croup and his foot on one of its hoofs, he bears down upon it, pressing it against the earth; and grasping it by the nostrils with one hand, with the other he plunges a knife into its flank. The impetuosity of this animated scene throws into high relief the agility and strength of the invincible hero. On the other hand, the suffering of the moribund victim gasping its last, with its limbs contracted in the spasms of death, the singular

---

*Compare my large work, *Textes et Monuments figurés relatifs aux Mystères de Mithra*, Vol. II., pp. 180 *et seq.*

mixture of exaltation and remorse depicted in
the countenance of its slayer, give prominence
to the pathetic side of this sacred drama, and
even to-day inspire in the heart of the spectator an emotion which the faithful of old experienced in all its living power. (See Fig.
44 and also the cover-stamp of this book.)

The traditional type of torch-bearers, or
dadophori, was not susceptible of a similar im-
passioned treatment. But one remarks, nevertheless, in the best specimens the advantageous
effect which the artist has produced by the
ample Phrygian garments and by emphasizing
the different emotions of hope and sadness
portrayed on the countenances of the two
young men. We possess a remarkable reproduction of this divine couple in the two statues
discovered near the Tiber, which Zoëga attributed to the epoch of Hadrian and which were
possibly imported from the Orient to Italy.*
(See Figures 47 and 48.) It will be seen how
their author succeeded in offsetting the
defective symmetry resulting from the fact
that the two figures, which are intended as
counterparts, have both their mantles fastened
at the right shoulder and falling down at the
right side.

The solicitous concern for details which
characterizes the works of the Antonine epoch
was also bestowed with more or less felicity

---

* *T. et M.*, Mon. 27, Plate II, opposite p. 209, Vol. II.
Conmut thinks these statues are prior to Hadrian.

upon the monuments of a slightly more recent
date.   Consider the group of Ostia, which

Fig. 47.

MITHRAIC DADOPHORUS.

Wrongly restored as Paris.

dates from the reign of Commodus, or the bas-
relief of the Villa Albani, which appears to be

contemporaneous with the first.* The artist
delighted in multiplying the folds of the gar-

Fig. 48.
MITHRAIC DADOPHORUS.
Wrongly restored as Paris.

ments and in increasing the undulations of the
hair merely to show his skill in conquering the

* *T. et M.*, Mon. 79, Fig. 67; and Mon. 38, Fig. 45.

difficulties which he had himself created; yet
even this *bizarre* mannerism does not atone
for the coldness of the total impression. The
success of this minute execution of details is
more felicitous in fragments of smaller dimensions. A small marble recently discovered in
Aquileia, and reproduced in our Frontispiece
is distinguished in this respect by a "bewilder-
ing cleverness of technique." The delicately
carved figures are almost entirely severed from
their massive base, to which they are attached
only by the thinnest supports. It is a piece of
artistic braggadocio in which the sculptor
parades his virtuosity by producing with a brit-
tle material the same effects that are obtained
by workers in ductile metals.*

But these comparatively perfect compositions are rare in Italy and especially so in the
provinces, and it has to be acknowledged that
the great mass of the Mithraic monuments is
of discouraging mediocrity. The hewers and

---

*M. von Schneider, *loc. cit.*, Vol. II., p. 488, who sees in
this composition "*ein verblüffendes technisches Geschick*,"
compares it with the relief on the base of the Antonine column
(Brunn, *Denkmäler gr. u. röm. Skulptur*, Pl. 210*b*), and a bas-
relief of the Campo Santo of Pisa (Dütschke, *Bildwerke in
Ober-Italien*, I., No. 60), and the bust of Commodus in the
Palais des Conservateurs (Helbig, *Führer*, second ed., No.
524). The same application of the technique of metal-work-
ing to marble may be noticed in two admirably preserved busts
which were discovered at Smyrna and are to-day to be found
in the Museum at Brussels (*Catal. des antiquitées acquises
par les musées royaux depuis le 1re janvier 1900*, Bruxelles,
1901, Nos. 110-111).

cutters of stone—they deserve no other name —who are responsible for these productions, were often content with roughly outlining by a few strokes of the chisel the scene which they pretended to reproduce. A garish coloring then emphasized certain details. The work is sometimes so hastily executed that the contours alone are distinctly marked, as in the hieroglyphics. It sufficed, it is true, merely to outline representations, the meaning of which every faithful devotee knew and which he completed in imagination; and it is our ignorance that feels so vividly the imperfections of these awkward and vague compositions. Still, some of the smaller bas-reliefs could never have been more than downright caricatures bordering on the grotesque, and their deformities strongly remind us of the little toy gingerbread men which are sold at our fairs.

The carelessness with which these tablets were executed is excused by their places of destination. The mystics of Mithra were wont not only to consecrate them in their temples, but also to adorn with them their modest dwelling-houses. This domestic consumption explains the enormous quantity of these monuments, which have been found wherever the cult penetrated. To satisfy the incessant demand of the faithful for these figures, the workshops in which they were carved must have produced them rapidly and in quantities.

The manufacturers of this brummagem sculpture had no other thought than that of cheaply satisfying their clientage of devotees, whose artistic tastes were far from exacting. The ancient manufacturers turned out hundreds of smaller tauroctonous Mithras,* just as our image-makers multiply in profusion the very same type of crucifixes and the very same Virgin Mary. It was the religious imagery of the epoch, and it was not more æsthetic than is ours to-day.

These manufacturers did not restrict themselves to the unceasing production of replicas of the same traditional type; they sought to diversify their wares, in order to recommend them to all tastes and purses. Look only at the series of ex-votos found in the mithræum of Sarmizegetusa in Dacia.† We find here specimens of all the models that the workshops of the place reproduced. High reliefs, which are difficult and costly, are avoided. At most, the marble was perforated in places, so as to show forth the group of the tauroctonous god. But what a wondrous variety in the small bas-reliefs which were affixed to the walls of the sanctuaries! For a mere bagatelle square tablets could be obtained bearing only

---

* The absence of machinery naturally excluded any absolute resemblance, but some of our bas-reliefs are certainly from the same hand or at least from the same workshop. *Cf. T. et M.*, Vol. II., Mon. 45 and 46; Figs. 85 and 95, Fig. 87; 192 and 192 *bis*; 194 and 195.

† *T. et M.*, Vol. II., Nos. 138 to 183.

the immolation of the bull. Sometimes its value is enhanced by the addition of a sort of predella, divided into three or four smaller scenes. Again, its composition is complicated by an upper panel decorated with accessory scenes. These, finally, also occupy the borders of the monuments, and encompass on four sides the principal representation. Again, the fancy of the workman taking flight, the tauroctonous god has been enclosed in a circle ornamented with the signs of the Zodiac, or in a crown of foliage. Frames were added or omitted. Considerable ingenuity was exercised to give new forms to the sculptured plaques. They were indiscriminately square, oblong, semicircular, trapezoidal, or even round. There are no two of these pieces which are exactly alike.

If these commercial products of labor for hire have only the remotest relationship with art, they nevertheless furnish a valuable commentary upon the stone-hewing industry of antiquity. We have many proofs that a goodly portion of the sculptures intended for the provincial cities were executed during the imperial epoch at Rome.* This is probably the case with some of the monuments discovered in Gaul, and also for those which adorned a mithræum in London.† On the other hand, certain statues discovered in the capital were

---

* Friedländer, *Sittengeschichte*, Vol. III., p. 280.

† *T. et M.*, Vol. II., Mon. 267 and the note on p. 390.

presumably imported from Asia Minor.* The
beautiful bas-reliefs of Virunum were likewise
brought from abroad, probably by way of
Aquileia. We know by the passion of the
Four Crowned Ones the importance of the
quarries of Pannonia in the third century,†
where marble was not only quarried but
worked. These stone-yards appear to have
been an important center for the manufacture
of Mithraic votive offerings. In any event,
there are several of them, exhumed in the
temples of Germany, which were unquestionably sculptured on the banks of the Danube.
These facts cast an interesting light on the
traffic in church ornaments during the days of
paganism.

Yet the majority of the Mithraic monuments
were undoubtedly executed on the spot. The
matter is clear for those which were sculptured
on the walls of natural rocks smoothed for the
purpose,—they are unfortunately all greatly
damaged,—but the proof of local manufacture
for many others is also forcibly forthcoming
from the nature of the stone employed. The
construction of these fragments likewise

---

* *T. et M.*, Vol. II., Mon. 235 and the note on p. 338. *Cf.*
supra, p. 122, Fig. 26.

† Wattenbach, *Passio sanct, quatuor coronat.*, with the
notes of Benndorf and Max Büdinger, 1870; *cf.* Friedländer,
op. cit., p. 282. A new text has been published by Wattenbach, *Sitzungsb. Akad.*, *Berlin*, XLVII., 1896, p. 1281 *et seq.*
There still exists of this work an unpublished Greek translation; *cf. Analecta Bollandiana*, XVI., 1897, p. 337.

clearly reveals that they are not the handi-
work of foreign masters and of some great
center of art, nor even of those nomadic sculptors who traversed the land in quest of lucrative or honorific employment, but of the
modest stone-cutters of some neighboring
town.

The local origin of the largest monuments
is best established, since their transportation
would have involved both numerous risks and
extravagant expenditures. Our collection of
large Mithraic bas-reliefs thus constitutes a
highly interesting group for the study of the
provincial art of the empire. Like the mass
of votive tablets that have come down to us,
these sculptures, which were exhibited in the
apse of the temples for the adoration of the
faithful, are also far from being masterpieces
of art. But they were nevertheless not executed with the same carelessness, and we feel
in their presence that their authors bestowed
upon them their best energies. If the artists
afforded no proof of originality in the inven-
tion of subjects, they nevertheless give evidence of ingenuity in the arrangement of their
figures and of their skill in handling the
material.

It must not be forgotten, further, in judging
of these fragments, that the painter came to
the aid of the sculptor and that the brush
completed what the chisel had only sketched.
On the naked marble or on stone coated with

plaster, flaring colors were laid: green, blue, yellow, black, and all shades of red were wantonly intermingled. This glaring contrast of tones accentuated the main contours of the figures, and made prominent their secondary parts. In many cases the details were only indicated with the brush. Gilding, finally, emphasized certain subsidiary features. In the penumbral darkness of the subterranean crypts, the reliefs of these sculptured compositions would have been almost invisible without this brilliant polychromatic vesture. Vivid variety of coloring, moreover, was one of the traditions of Oriental art, and Lucian had already contrasted the simple and graceful forms of the Hellenic deities with the ostentatious gaudery of the gods imported from Asia.*

The most remarkable of these sculptures have been brought to light in the north of Gaul, or, more precisely, on the Rhenish frontier. It appears that we must attribute this entire group of monuments to that interesting school of sculpture which flourished in Belgium in the second and third centuries, the productions of which unquestionably surpass those of the workshops of the south. One cannot contemplate the bas-relief of Osterburken, which is the most complete of the series, without being impressed with the wealth and the general harmony of this vast composition. The

* Lucian, *Jup. trag.*, §8.

confused impression resulting from the accu-
mulation of personages and groups,—a defect
which the Mithraic monuments show with
many others of their epoch, and especially
with the sarcophagi, the composition of which
is generally intricate,—is here tempered by the
judicious use of separating bands and frames.
If we were anxious to criticize the details of
these works, it would be easy to point out the
disproportion of certain of their figures, the
awkwardness of certain of their movements,
and sometimes the stiffness of their attitudes
and vestments. But these defects should not
render us oblivious to the delicacy of the work
here performed with a crumbling material,
and especially to the praiseworthy success with
which a conception of real grandeur has been
realized. To attempt to represent on stone
not only the gods but the cosmogony of the
Mysteries and the episodes of the legend of
Mithra, even to the final immolation of the
bull, was an undertaking attended with great
perils and is a meritorious achievement even
in partial success. Even prior to this date,
and particularly on the sarcophagi, instances
occur where the successive moments of the
drama are depicted on superposed or parallel
plates, but we cannot, nevertheless, cite a single monument of Roman paganism which can
be compared in this respect to our grand bas-
reliefs, and for similar productions we must
wait for the lengthy compositions with which

the Christian mosaicists decorated the walls of their churches.

We shall not inquire here into the origin of each one of the different representations which are portrayed upon our monuments; we shall merely observe that in spite of their variety two or even three clearly marked classes may be distinguished. Some of the figures have been borrowed outright from the traditional types of Græco-Roman art. Ahura-Mazda destroying the monsters that had risen against him is a Hellenic Zeus annihilating the giants with his bolts; Verethragna is transformed into a Hercules; Helios is a young man with long flowing hair, mounted on the usual quadriga; Neptune, Venus, Diana, Mercury, Mars, Pluto, Saturn, are shown to us in their ordinary aspect with the garb and attributes which are known to have been theirs from time immemorial. Similarly, the Winds, the Seasons, and the Planets had been personified long before the propagation of Mithraism, and the latter cult had only to reproduce in its temples the models that had long since been made popular.

On the other hand, one personage at least is a transformation of an Asiatic archetype; this is the leontocephalous, or lion-headed, Kronos. (See Figs. 20–23.) Like the majority of his compeers, this animal-headed monster is a creation of the Oriental imagination. His genealogy would doubtless carry us back to

Fig. 49.

MITHRAIC KRONOS, OR PERSONIFICATION OF INFINITE
TIME.

Surrounded by the signs of the Zodiac (see p. 121). In the
corners the gods of the Winds. Here represented without the
head of a lion, which appears on the breast of the figure.
A Roman beautification of the horrific features of the Oriental
god. (Bas-relief of Modena, *Rev. arch.*, 1902, I., p. 1.)   223

the period of Assyrian sculpture. But the
artists of the Occident, having to represent a
deity entirely strange to the Greek Pantheon,
and being untrammelled by the traditions of
any school, gave free rein to their fancy. The
various transformations to which they subjected his figure were in part influenced by
religious considerations, which tended to com-
plicate the symbolism of this deified abstrac-
tion and to multiply more and more his
attributes, and in part by an æsthetic solicitude
to soften as much as possible the monstrous
character of this barbaric personage, and thus
gradually to humanize it. Ultimately they
suppressed the lion's head, and contented
themselves with representing this animal by
its feet only, or with placing the head of the
beast on the figure's breast. (See Fig. 49.)

The leontocephalous god of Eternity is the
most original creation of Mithraic art, and if it
is totally destitute of the charm of grace, its
unwonted aspect and the suggestive accumu-
lation of its attributes awakened curiosity and
provoked reflection. With the exception of
this god of Time, we can establish the Oriental origin of certain emblems only, like the
Phrygian bonnet topping a staff, or the sphere
surmounted by an eagle representing the
Heavens. As the Mithra immolating the bull,
so also the other scenes in which this hero
appears as actor, are unquestionably in greater
part the transpositions of *motifs* popular in the

Hellenistic epoch, although we are unable in every case to rediscover the original which the Roman marble-cutter imitated or the elements which he combined in his composition. As for the rest, the artistic value of these

Fig. 50.
BIRTH OF ERICHTHONIOS.
From a Greek vase. (Baumeister.)

adaptations is generally very slight. We have only to compare the lifeless group of Mithra issuing from the rock (Fig. 30) with the animated picture of the birth of Erichthonios as it is portrayed on Greek vases (see, for example, Fig. 50) to note the superior artistic effect which the ancient Hellenic ceramists could produce from a similar theme. The poverty of the innovations which the Mithraic iconography introduced contrasts painfully with the importance of the religious movement that provoked them. We have, in this, an additional corroboration of the fact that in the epoch in which the Persian Mysteries spread throughout the empire, the ancient sculpture was doomed beyond recall. Whereas, during the Hellenistic period, sculptors were still able to conceive new forms felicitously adapted to the character of the Egyptian divinities, under the empire, on the other hand, the majority of the Mazdean gods, despite their very peculiar nature, were compelled, whether or no, to take on the form and the garb of the denizens of Olympus. And if for some of these strange subjects new types were actually invented, they were in every instance distressingly commonplace. The superabundant wealth inherited from the ancient generations had enervated the generative potencies of art; and, accustomed to draw from these rich stores, art had grown incapable of all individual productivity.

But we should be wrong in exacting from the adepts of Mithraism something which they never made the pretense of offering. The religion which they preached was not a cult of beauty, and love of plastic form would doubtless have appeared to them a vain, if not a condemnable, taste. Religious emotion alone was of consequence in their eyes, and to awaken it they addressed themselves mainly to the reason. In spite of the many appropriations which it made from the treasury of types created by Greek sculptors, Mithraic art rested at heart Asiatic, like the Mysteries of which it was the expression. Its predominating idea was not to provoke an æsthetic impression; it aimed not to fascinate, but to tell its mission and to instruct,—faithful in this also to the traditions of the ancient Orient. The jumbled mass of personages and groups which are presented on some of the bas-reliefs, the host of attributes with which it surcharged the eternal Kronos,* show us that a new ideal was born with the new religion. These uncouth and unappealing symbols, the manifold use of which our monuments exhibit, did not allure by their elegance or nobility; they fascinated the mind by the disquieting attractions of the Unknown, and provoked in souls reverential fear for an august mystery.

Thus is explained why this art, extremely refined despite its imperfections, exercised a lasting influence. It was united to Christian art by an affinity of nature, and the symbolism which it had popularized in the Occident did not perish with it. Even the allegorical figures of the cosmic cycle which the devotees of the Persian god had reproduced in great profusion (for nature was for them divine throughout) were adopted by Christianity,

* *Cf.* p. 139, Fig. 35, and p. 105 *et seq.*

although in essence they were diametrically
opposed to its spirit. So with the images of
the Heavens, the Earth, and the Ocean, of the
Sun, the Moon, and the Planets, and of the
signs of the Zodiac, of the Winds, the Seasons,
and the Elements, so frequent on the Christian sarcophagi, the mosaics, and miniatures.

The mediocre compositions which the artists had conceived to represent the episodes
of the legend of Mithra appeared also worthy
of imitation to the Christian ages, which were
even more powerless than their predecessors
to shake off the traditions of the workshops.
When, after the triumph of the Church, Christian sculptors were confronted with subjects
hitherto unattempted, and found themselves
under the embarrassing obligations of depict-
ing on stone the personages and stories of the
Bible, they were happy in the opportunity of
being able to draw inspiration from the por-
trayals which the Persian Mysteries had popularized. A few alterations in costume and
attitude transformed a pagan scene into a
Christian picture. Mithra discharging his
arrows against the rock became Moses causing
the waters of the mountain of Horeb to gush
forth; the Sun, raising his ally out of the
Ocean, served to express the ascension of
Elijah in the chariot of fire; and to the time
of the Middle Ages the type of the tauroctonous god was perpetuated in the images of
Samson rending the lion.

INDEX

A

Absolutism, theory of, 90, 103.

Abstinence, 160.

Adam-Klissi, 43.

Adige, river, 73.

Adriatic, Mithraism along the coasts of the, 67.

Æon, 105 et seq. (See *Kronos.*)

Agri Decumates, 52, 83, 199.

Ahriman, 7, 112, 137, 140; the destruction of the world by, 146.

Ahura-Mazda, 5 et seq., 20, 27, 94, 113, 222.

Alexander the Great, 12, 20, 192.

Alexandria, 92.

Alps, Mithraism in defiles of the, 72.

Amshaspands, 2, 5.

Anâhita, 8 et seq., 10, 20, 179 et seq.

Anaïtis, 112.

Anangke, 111.

Anauni, tribe of the, 206.

Animal disguises, 153.

Animals and stars, 122.

Antiochus of Commagene, 13, 14, 26, 27, 95.

Apathy, stoic, 161.

Apotheosis of the emperors, 90 et seq.

Apuleius, 164.

Apulum, 45, 139.

Aquileia, Mithraism in, 67 et seq., 73, 213.

Aquincum, 46.

Arcana, the secrecy of the, 172.

Archer, the divine, 138, 197, 228.

Arete, 112.

Aristocracy and Mithraism, the Roman, 81 et seq., 205.

Ark, 138.

Armenia, Mithraism in, 16.

Armenians, religion of the, 16.

Army, the principal agent of the diffusion of the Mithraic religion, 40 et seq.

Arshtât, 5.

Artagnes, 111.

Artaxerxes, 8, 9.

Artemis Tauropolos, 20.

Art, Mithraic, 24, 209 et seq.; intricacy of, 221; symbolism of, 227; its influence on Christian sculpture, 196; Christianity adopts symbols of, 228.

Art of the empire, provincial, 219.

Ascension, Mithraic, 194.

Asceticism, 141.

Asha, 112.

Ashi-Vañuhi, 5.

Asia Minor, Mithraism in, 11 et seq.; resists the civilization of Rome, 35.

Asia Propria, 79

Asia, religions of, and the Cæsars, 91.

Astarte at Rome, 34.

Astrolatry, 10.

Centurions, a microcosm of the empire, 40, 41.
Ceramists, Hellenic, 225.
Ceremonial, the occult, 162 et seq.
Chaldæans, theology of the, 10; as astrologers, 78, 85; theories, influence of their, 119.
Chester, 57.
Chosroes, vi.
Christ, 193, 195.
Christianity, battle between idolatry and, iii et seq.; struggle between Mithraism and, 188 et seq.; resemblances between Mithraism and, 193; differences between Mithraism and, 197; adopts symbols of Mithraic art, 228.
Christians, persecutions of, 200.
Christmas, 167, 191, 196, 202.
Chrysostomos, Dion, 25.
Church ornaments during the days of paganism, 218.
Cilicia, pirates of, 31, 35, 37, 42.
Clergy, Mithraic, 150 et seq., 165.
Cologne, 52.
Coloring of Mithraic statues, 219.
Colt, title of, 153.
Commagene, 41, 43, 178.
Commandments of Mithraism, 140.
Commerce, international, 79.
Commodus, 38, 83, 87, 97, 212.
Communion, the Mithraic, 158 et seq., 194.
Compromise, Mithraic policy of, 198.
Conflagration, 138.
Congregations, Mithraic, 169.

Constantine, 200.
Constantius, 201.
Constellations, worship of the Planets and the, 148.
Continence, 141.
Conventicles, the Mithraic, 171.
Corbulo, 47.
Creator, Mithra the, 137.
Crown, the, 156.
Ctesias, 9.
Cybele, 17, 30, 87, 112, 179.

D

Dacia, Mithraism in, 44 et seq., 139, 199.
Dadophori, 57. (See *Torch-bearers.*)
Dalmatia, 40, 76.
Danube, 44, 51.
Darkness, the Spirit of, and his pestilential scourges, 137.
Day and night, struggle between, 4.
Dead, resurrection of the, 191.
Dea Syria at Rome, 35.
Deities, sidereal, 120; septuple division of the, 155.
Deliverance, 143.
Deluge, 138.
Despotism, 90, 91 et seq.
Destiny, 95, 109, 110, 124.
Devotees, Mithraic, 150 et seq.
Diadochi, Mithraism and the, 11 et seq.
Diana, 112.
Diocletian, vi, 48, 89, 98, 200.
Dioscuri, the, 123 et seq.
Disc, the radiant, 100.
Divine flame, 26.
Dog of Mithra, the, 135, 137.
Dolichenum, 178.

31; analysis of the constituent elements of, 30; Semitic theories in, 10; religious survivals in, 30; struggle between Christianity and, v, 188 et seq.; resemblances between Christianity and, 193; differences between Christianity and, 197; dissemination of, in the Roman Empire, 33 et seq.; army principal agent of diffusion of, 40 et seq., 60, 77, 78; disseminated by Syrian merchants and slaves, 61 et seq., 63 et seq., 69, 74 et seq., 78; imperial officers disseminated, 74 et seq.; the Roman aristocracy and, 81 et seq., 205; the imperial power of Rome and, 85 et seq.; reasons the Roman Empire supported it, 88 et seq.; despotism and, 91 et seq.; favored the pretensions of the Cæsars, 101; dogmatology of, tended to lift princes above the level of humankind, 102; at its apogee, 15, 84 et seq., 88 et seq., 177, 199; the doctrines of, 104 et seq.; its theology, 105 et seq.; astrology and, 125; its liturgy, clergy and devotees, 150 et seq.; the religions of the empire and, 175 et seq.; importance of its history, vi; philosophy and, 25; the Stoic philosophy and, 25; excluded from the Hellenic world, 33; Roman tolerance of, 85; associated with the religion of the *Magna Mater*

(Great Mother), 86 et seq.; legal status of, 86; sacred poetry of, 126; commandments of, 140; a religion of soldiers, 142; satisfied the hearts of the simple-minded, 148; allurements of, 149; conforms religion to ancient science, 149; offers opportunities for prayer and motives for veneration, 149; the religious expression of the physics and astronomy of the Roman world, 149; admission to, 156; stupendous illusions of, 173; women and, 173; its priests, 175; its policy of compromise, 198; its temples sacked, 199, 203; downfall of, 203 et seq.; its art, sculpture, etc., 209 et seq.; monuments of, 43 et seq., 209 et seq.; not a cult of beauty, 226.

Mithrakana, the, 9, 167.
Mithridates, 13.
Mithridates Eupator, 31.
Mitra-Varuna, 2.
Mœsia, Mithraism in, 40, 43, 74.
Monachism, Mithraic, 165.
Monarchical power, Mazdean ideas concerning, 95.
Monarchs, majesty of, sacred, 93.
Monotheism, 187, 188.
Moon, worship of the, 119.
Mosaicists, Christian, 222.
Moses, 197, 228.
Mothers, order of, 179.
Mother, the Great, 19. (See *Mater, Magna.*)

Vendidad, the, 26.
Venus, 112, 181.
Venusia, 71.
Verethraghna, 5, 20, 127, 222.
Vespasian, 46, 47, 77.
Veterans disseminate Mithraism, 77.
Vienna, 49.
Villa Albani, 212.
Virunum, 50, 73, 113, 199, 218.
Vulcan, 112, 114.

W

Water, 114.
West, 7.
Winds, the, 197, 222, 223.
Witchcraft, 125.
Women in Mithraism, 173.

World, origin and destiny of the, 109, 120, 140.

Y

Yazatas, 5 et seq., 175
York, 57.

Z

Zeno, 25.
Zervan, 105 et seq., 125. (See *Kronos*.)
Zeus, 111, 222; Ahura-Mazda and, 20.
Zodiac, signs of the, 109, 121 et seq., 153, 223.
Zoroaster, 152.
Zoroastrianism, 2 et seq., 8, 165. (See *Mithraism*.)

A CATALOGUE OF SELECTED DOVER BOOKS
IN ALL FIELDS OF INTEREST

A CATALOGUE OF SELECTED DOVER BOOKS
IN ALL FIELDS OF INTEREST

AMERICA'S OLD MASTERS, James T. Flexner. Four men emerged unexpectedly from provincial 18th century America to leadership in European art: Benjamin West, J. S. Copley, C. R. Peale, Gilbert Stuart. Brilliant coverage of lives and contributions. Revised, 1967 edition. 69 plates. 365pp. of text.

21806-6 Paperbound $3.00

FIRST FLOWERS OF OUR WILDERNESS: AMERICAN PAINTING, THE COLONIAL PERIOD, James T. Flexner. Painters, and regional painting traditions from earliest Colonial times up to the emergence of Copley, West and Peale Sr., Foster, Gustavus Hesselius, Feke, John Smibert and many anonymous painters in the primitive manner. Engaging presentation, with 162 illustrations. xxii + 368pp.

22180-6 Paperbound $3.50

THE LIGHT OF DISTANT SKIES: AMERICAN PAINTING, 1760-1835, James T. Flexner. The great generation of early American painters goes to Europe to learn and to teach: West, Copley, Gilbert Stuart and others. Allston, Trumbull, Morse; also contemporary American painters—primitives, derivatives, academics—who remained in America. 102 illustrations. xiii + 306pp. 22179-2 Paperbound $3.50

A HISTORY OF THE RISE AND PROGRESS OF THE ARTS OF DESIGN IN THE UNITED STATES, William Dunlap. Much the richest mine of information on early American painters, sculptors, architects, engravers, miniaturists, etc. The only source of information for scores of artists, the major primary source for many others. Unabridged reprint of rare original 1834 edition, with new introduction by James T. Flexner, and 394 new illustrations. Edited by Rita Weiss. 6⅝ x 9⅝.

21695-0, 21696-9, 21697-7 Three volumes, Paperbound $13.50

EPOCHS OF CHINESE AND JAPANESE ART, Ernest F. Fenollosa. From primitive Chinese art to the 20th century, thorough history, explanation of every important art period and form, including Japanese woodcuts; main stress on China and Japan, but Tibet, Korea also included. Still unexcelled for its detailed, rich coverage of cultural background, aesthetic elements, diffusion studies, particularly of the historical period. 2nd, 1913 edition. 242 illustrations. lii + 439pp. of text.

20364-6, 20365-4 Two volumes, Paperbound $6.00

THE GENTLE ART OF MAKING ENEMIES, James A. M. Whistler. Greatest wit of his day deflates Oscar Wilde, Ruskin, Swinburne; strikes back at inane critics, exhibitions, art journalism; aesthetics of impressionist revolution in most striking form. Highly readable classic by great painter. Reproduction of edition designed by Whistler. Introduction by Alfred Werner. xxxvi + 334pp.

21875-9 Paperbound $2.50

VISUAL ILLUSIONS: THEIR CAUSES, CHARACTERISTICS, AND APPLICATIONS, Matthew Luckiesh. Thorough description and discussion of optical illusion, geometric and perspective, particularly; size and shape distortions, illusions of color, of motion; natural illusions; use of illusion in art and magic, industry, etc. Most useful today with op art, also for classical art. Scores of effects illustrated. Introduction by William H. Ittleson. 100 illustrations. xxi + 252pp.
21530-X Paperbound $2.00

A HANDBOOK OF ANATOMY FOR ART STUDENTS, Arthur Thomson. Thorough, virtually exhaustive coverage of skeletal structure, musculature, etc. Full text, supplemented by anatomical diagrams and drawings and by photographs of undraped figures. Unique in its comparison of male and female forms, pointing out differences of contour, texture, form. 211 figures, 40 drawings, 86 photographs. xx + 459pp.
5⅜ x 8⅜. 21163-0 Paperbound $3.50

150 MASTERPIECES OF DRAWING, Selected by Anthony Toney. Full page reproductions of drawings from the early 16th to the end of the 18th century, all beautifully reproduced: Rembrandt, Michelangelo, Dürer, Fragonard, Urs, Graf, Wouwerman, many others. First-rate browsing book, model book for artists. xviii + 150pp.
8⅜ x 11¼. 21032-4 Paperbound $2.50

THE LATER WORK OF AUBREY BEARDSLEY, Aubrey Beardsley. Exotic, erotic, ironic masterpieces in full maturity: Comedy Ballet, Venus and Tannhauser, Pierrot, Lysistrata, Rape of the Lock, Savoy material, Ali Baba, Volpone, etc. This material revolutionized the art world, and is still powerful, fresh, brilliant. With *The Early Work,* all Beardsley's finest work. 174 plates, 2 in color. xiv + 176pp. 8⅛ x 11.
21817-1 Paperbound $3.00

DRAWINGS OF REMBRANDT, Rembrandt van Rijn. Complete reproduction of fabulously rare edition by Lippmann and Hofstede de Groot, completely reedited, updated, improved by Prof. Seymour Slive, Fogg Museum. Portraits, Biblical sketches, landscapes, Oriental types, nudes, episodes from classical mythology—All Rembrandt's fertile genius. Also selection of drawings by his pupils and followers. "Stunning volumes," *Saturday Review.* 550 illustrations. lxxviii + 552pp.
9⅛ x 12¼. 21485-0, 21486-9 Two volumes, Paperbound $10.00

THE DISASTERS OF WAR, Francisco Goya. One of the masterpieces of Western civilization—83 etchings that record Goya's shattering, bitter reaction to the Napoleonic war that swept through Spain after the insurrection of 1808 and to war in general. Reprint of the first edition, with three additional plates from Boston's Museum of Fine Arts. All plates facsimile size. Introduction by Philip Hofer, Fogg Museum.
v + 97pp. 9⅜ x 8¼. 21872-4 Paperbound $2.00

GRAPHIC WORKS OF ODILON REDON. Largest collection of Redon's graphic works ever assembled: 172 lithographs, 28 etchings and engravings, 9 drawings. These include some of his most famous works. All the plates from *Odilon Redon: oeuvre graphique complet,* plus additional plates. New introduction and caption translations by Alfred Werner. 209 illustrations. xxvii + 209pp. 9⅛ x 12¼.
21966-8 Paperbound $4.00

DESIGN BY ACCIDENT; A BOOK OF "ACCIDENTAL EFFECTS" FOR ARTISTS AND DESIGNERS, James F. O'Brien. Create your own unique, striking, imaginative effects by "controlled accident" interaction of materials: paints and lacquers, oil and water based paints, splatter, crackling materials, shatter, similar items. Everything you do will be different; first book on this limitless art, so useful to both fine artist and commercial artist. Full instructions. 192 plates showing "accidents," 8 in color. viii + 215pp. 8⅜ x 11¼. 21942-9 Paperbound $3.50

THE BOOK OF SIGNS, Rudolf Koch. Famed German type designer draws 493 beautiful symbols: religious, mystical, alchemical, imperial, property marks, runes, etc. Remarkable fusion of traditional and modern. Good for suggestions of timelessness, smartness, modernity. Text. vi + 104pp. 6⅛ x 9¼.

20162-7 Paperbound $1.25

HISTORY OF INDIAN AND INDONESIAN ART, Ananda K. Coomaraswamy. An unabridged republication of one of the finest books by a great scholar in Eastern art. Rich in descriptive material, history, social backgrounds; Sunga reliefs, Rajput paintings, Gupta temples, Burmese frescoes, textiles, jewelry, sculpture, etc. 400 photos. viii + 423pp. 6⅜ x 9¾. 21436-2 Paperbound $5.00

PRIMITIVE ART, Franz Boas. America's foremost anthropologist surveys textiles, ceramics, woodcarving, basketry, metalwork, etc.; patterns, technology, creation of symbols, style origins. All areas of world, but very full on Northwest Coast Indians. More than 350 illustrations of baskets, boxes, totem poles, weapons, etc. 378 pp. 20025-6 Paperbound $3.00

THE GENTLEMAN AND CABINET MAKER'S DIRECTOR, Thomas Chippendale. Full reprint (third edition, 1762) of most influential furniture book of all time, by master cabinetmaker. 200 plates, illustrating chairs, sofas, mirrors, tables, cabinets, plus 24 photographs of surviving pieces. Biographical introduction by N. Bienenstock. vi + 249pp. 9⅞ x 12¾. 21601-2 Paperbound $4.00

AMERICAN ANTIQUE FURNITURE, Edgar G. Miller, Jr. The basic coverage of all American furniture before 1840. Individual chapters cover type of furniture—clocks, tables, sideboards, etc.—chronologically, with inexhaustible wealth of data. More than 2100 photographs, all identified, commented on. Essential to all early American collectors. Introduction by H. E. Keyes. vi + 1106pp. 7⅞ x 10¾. 21599-7, 21600-4 Two volumes, Paperbound $11.00

PENNSYLVANIA DUTCH AMERICAN FOLK ART, Henry J. Kauffman. 279 photos, 28 drawings of tulipware, Fraktur script, painted tinware, toys, flowered furniture, quilts, samplers, hex signs, house interiors, etc. Full descriptive text. Excellent for tourist, rewarding for designer, collector. Map. 146pp. 7⅞ x 10¾.

21205-X Paperbound $2.50

EARLY NEW ENGLAND GRAVESTONE RUBBINGS, Edmund V. Gillon, Jr. 43 photographs, 226 carefully reproduced rubbings show heavily symbolic, sometimes macabre early gravestones, up to early 19th century. Remarkable early American primitive art, occasionally strikingly beautiful; always powerful. Text. xxvi + 207pp. 8⅜ x 11¼. 21380-3 Paperbound $3.50

ALPHABETS AND ORNAMENTS, Ernst Lehner. Well-known pictorial source for decorative alphabets, script examples, cartouches, frames, decorative title pages, calligraphic initials, borders, similar material. 14th to 19th century, mostly European. Useful in almost any graphic arts designing, varied styles. 750 illustrations. 256pp. 7 x 10.   21905-4 Paperbound $4.00

PAINTING: A CREATIVE APPROACH, Norman Colquhoun. For the beginner simple guide provides an instructive approach to painting: major stumbling blocks for beginner; overcoming them, technical points; paints and pigments; oil painting; watercolor and other media and color. New section on "plastic" paints. Glossary. Formerly *Paint Your Own Pictures.* 221pp.   22000-1 Paperbound $1.75

THE ENJOYMENT AND USE OF COLOR, Walter Sargent. Explanation of the relations between colors themselves and between colors in nature and art, including hundreds of little-known facts about color values, intensities, effects of high and low illumination, complementary colors. Many practical hints for painters, references to great masters. 7 color plates, 29 illustrations. x + 274pp.
                                                                                                    20944-X Paperbound $2.75

THE NOTEBOOKS OF LEONARDO DA VINCI, compiled and edited by Jean Paul Richter. 1566 extracts from original manuscripts reveal the full range of Leonardo's versatile genius: all his writings on painting, sculpture, architecture, anatomy, astronomy, geography, topography, physiology, mining, music, etc., in both Italian and English, with 186 plates of manuscript pages and more than 500 additional drawings. Includes studies for the Last Supper, the lost Sforza monument, and other works. Total of xlvii + 866pp. $7\frac{7}{8}$ x $10\frac{3}{4}$.
                                                    22572-0, 22573-9 Two volumes, Paperbound $10.00

MONTGOMERY WARD CATALOGUE OF 1895. Tea gowns, yards of flannel and pillow-case lace, stereoscopes, books of gospel hymns, the New Improved Singer Sewing Machine, side saddles, milk skimmers, straight-edged razors, high-button shoes, spittoons, and on and on . . . listing some 25,000 items, practically all illustrated. Essential to the shoppers of the 1890's, it is our truest record of the spirit of the period. Unaltered reprint of Issue No. 57, Spring and Summer 1895. Introduction by Boris Emmet. Innumerable illustrations. xiii + 624pp. $8\frac{1}{2}$ x $11\frac{5}{8}$.
                                                                                                    22377-9 Paperbound $6.95

THE CRYSTAL PALACE EXHIBITION ILLUSTRATED CATALOGUE (LONDON, 1851). One of the wonders of the modern world—the Crystal Palace Exhibition in which all the nations of the civilized world exhibited their achievements in the arts and sciences—presented in an equally important illustrated catalogue. More than 1700 items pictured with accompanying text—ceramics, textiles, cast-iron work, carpets, pianos, sleds, razors, wall-papers, billiard tables, beehives, silverware and hundreds of other artifacts—represent the focal point of Victorian culture in the Western World. Probably the largest collection of Victorian decorative art ever assembled— indispensable for antiquarians and designers. Unabridged republication of the Art-Journal Catalogue of the Great Exhibition of 1851, with all terminal essays. New introduction by John Gloag, F.S.A. xxxiv + 426pp. 9 x 12.
                                                                                                    22503-8 Paperbound $4.50

A History of Costume, Carl Köhler. Definitive history, based on surviving pieces of clothing primarily, and paintings, statues, etc. secondarily. Highly readable text, supplemented by 594 illustrations of costumes of the ancient Mediterranean peoples, Greece and Rome, the Teutonic prehistoric period; costumes of the Middle Ages, Renaissance, Baroque, 18th and 19th centuries. Clear, measured patterns are provided for many clothing articles. Approach is practical throughout. Enlarged by Emma von Sichart. 464pp. 21030-8 Paperbound $3.50

Oriental Rugs, Antique and Modern, Walter A. Hawley. A complete and authoritative treatise on the Oriental rug—where they are made, by whom and how, designs and symbols, characteristics in detail of the six major groups, how to distinguish them and how to buy them. Detailed technical data is provided on periods, weaves, warps, wefts, textures, sides, ends and knots, although no technical background is required for an understanding. 11 color plates, 80 halftones, 4 maps. vi + 320pp. 6⅛ x 9⅛. 22366-3 Paperbound $5.00

Ten Books on Architecture, Vitruvius. By any standards the most important book on architecture ever written. Early Roman discussion of aesthetics of building, construction methods, orders, sites, and every other aspect of architecture has inspired, instructed architecture for about 2,000 years. Stands behind Palladio, Michelangelo, Bramante, Wren, countless others. Definitive Morris H. Morgan translation. 68 illustrations. xii + 331pp. 20645-9 Paperbound $3.00

The Four Books of Architecture, Andrea Palladio. Translated into every major Western European language in the two centuries following its publication in 1570, this has been one of the most influential books in the history of architecture. Complete reprint of the 1738 Isaac Ware edition. New introduction by Adolf Placzek, Columbia Univ. 216 plates. xxii + 110pp. of text. 9½ x 12¾. 21308-0 Clothbound $10.00

Sticks and Stones: A Study of American Architecture and Civilization, Lewis Mumford.One of the great classics of American cultural history. American architecture from the medieval-inspired earliest forms to the early 20th century; evolution of structure and style, and reciprocal influences on environment. 21 photographic illustrations. 238pp. 20202-X Paperbound $2.00

The American Builder's Companion, Asher Benjamin. The most widely used early 19th century architectural style and source book, for colonial up into Greek Revival periods. Extensive development of geometry of carpentering, construction of sashes, frames, doors, stairs; plans and elevations of domestic and other buildings. Hundreds of thousands of houses were built according to this book, now invaluable to historians, architects, restorers, etc. 1827 edition. 59 plates. 114pp. 7⅞ x 10¾. 22236-5 Paperbound $3.50

Dutch Houses in the Hudson Valley Before 1776, Helen Wilkinson Reynolds. The standard survey of the Dutch colonial house and outbuildings, with constructional features, decoration, and local history associated with individual homesteads. Introduction by Franklin D. Roosevelt. Map. 150 illustrations. 469pp. 6⅝ x 9¼. 21469-9 Paperbound $4.00

THE ARCHITECTURE OF COUNTRY HOUSES, Andrew J. Downing. Together with Vaux's *Villas and Cottages* this is the basic book for Hudson River Gothic architecture of the middle Victorian period. Full, sound discussions of general aspects of housing, architecture, style, decoration, furnishing, together with scores of detailed house plans, illustrations of specific buildings, accompanied by full text. Perhaps the most influential single American architectural book. 1850 edition. Introduction by J. Stewart Johnson. 321 figures, 34 architectural designs. xvi + 560pp.

22003-6 Paperbound $4.00

LOST EXAMPLES OF COLONIAL ARCHITECTURE, John Mead Howells. Full-page photographs of buildings that have disappeared or been so altered as to be denatured, including many designed by major early American architects. 245 plates. xvii + 248pp. 7⅞ x 10¾.

21143-6 Paperbound $3.50

DOMESTIC ARCHITECTURE OF THE AMERICAN COLONIES AND OF THE EARLY REPUBLIC, Fiske Kimball. Foremost architect and restorer of Williamsburg and Monticello covers nearly 200 homes between 1620-1825. Architectural details, construction, style features, special fixtures, floor plans, etc. Generally considered finest work in its area. 219 illustrations of houses, doorways, windows, capital mantels. xx + 314pp. 7⅞ x 10¾.

21743-4 Paperbound $4.00

EARLY AMERICAN ROOMS: 1650-1858, edited by Russell Hawes Kettell. Tour of 12 rooms, each representative of a different era in American history and each furnished, decorated, designed and occupied in the style of the era. 72 plans and elevations, 8-page color section, etc., show fabrics, wall papers, arrangements, etc. Full descriptive text. xvii + 200pp. of text. 8⅜ x 11¼.

21633-0 Paperbound $5.00

THE FITZWILLIAM VIRGINAL BOOK, edited by J. Fuller Maitland and W. B. Squire. Full modern printing of famous early 17th-century ms. volume of 300 works by Morley, Byrd, Bull, Gibbons, etc. For piano or other modern keyboard instrument; easy to read format. xxxvi + 938pp. 8⅜ x 11.

21068-5, 21069-3 Two volumes, Paperbound $10.00

KEYBOARD MUSIC, Johann Sebastian Bach. Bach Gesellschaft edition. A rich selection of Bach's masterpieces for the harpsichord: the six English Suites, six French Suites, the six Partitas (Clavierübung part I), the Goldberg Variations (Clavierübung part IV), the fifteen Two-Part Inventions and the fifteen Three-Part Sinfonias. Clearly reproduced on large sheets with ample margins; eminently playable. vi + 312pp. 8⅛ x 11.

22360-4 Paperbound $5.00

THE MUSIC OF BACH: AN INTRODUCTION, Charles Sanford Terry. A fine, nontechnical introduction to Bach's music, both instrumental and vocal. Covers organ music, chamber music, passion music, other types. Analyzes themes, developments, innovations. x + 114pp.

21075-8 Paperbound $1.25

BEETHOVEN AND HIS NINE SYMPHONIES, Sir George Grove. Noted British musicologist provides best history, analysis, commentary on symphonies. Very thorough, rigorously accurate; necessary to both advanced student and amateur music lover. 436 musical passages. vii + 407 pp.

20334-4 Paperbound $2.75

JOHANN SEBASTIAN BACH, Philipp Spitta. One of the great classics of musicology, this definitive analysis of Bach's music (and life) has never been surpassed. Lucid, nontechnical analyses of hundreds of pieces (30 pages devoted to St. Matthew Passion, 26 to B Minor Mass). Also includes major analysis of 18th-century music. 450 musical examples. 40-page musical supplement. Total of xx + 1799pp.
(EUK) 22278-0, 22279-9 Two volumes, Clothbound $17.50

MOZART AND HIS PIANO CONCERTOS, Cuthbert Girdlestone. The only full-length study of an important area of Mozart's creativity. Provides detailed analyses of all 23 concertos, traces inspirational sources. 417 musical examples. Second edition. 509pp.
21271-8 Paperbound $3.50

THE PERFECT WAGNERITE: A COMMENTARY ON THE NIBLUNG'S RING, George Bernard Shaw. Brilliant and still relevant criticism in remarkable essays on Wagner's Ring cycle, Shaw's ideas on political and social ideology behind the plots, role of Leitmotifs, vocal requisites, etc. Prefaces. xxi + 136pp.
(USO) 21707-8 Paperbound $1.50

DON GIOVANNI, W. A. Mozart. Complete libretto, modern English translation; biographies of composer and librettist; accounts of early performances and critical reaction. Lavishly illustrated. All the material you need to understand and appreciate this great work. Dover Opera Guide and Libretto Series; translated and introduced by Ellen Bleiler. 92 illustrations. 209pp.
21134-7 Paperbound $2.00

HIGH FIDELITY SYSTEMS: A LAYMAN'S GUIDE, Roy F. Allison. All the basic information you need for setting up your own audio system: high fidelity and stereo record players, tape records, F.M. Connections, adjusting tone arm, cartridge, checking needle alignment, positioning speakers, phasing speakers, adjusting hums, trouble-shooting, maintenance, and similar topics. Enlarged 1965 edition. More than 50 charts, diagrams, photos. iv + 91pp.
21514-8 Paperbound $1.25

REPRODUCTION OF SOUND, Edgar Villchur. Thorough coverage for laymen of high fidelity systems, reproducing systems in general, needles, amplifiers, preamps, loudspeakers, feedback, explaining physical background. "A rare talent for making technicalities vividly comprehensible," R. Darrell, *High Fidelity*. 69 figures. iv + 92pp.
21515-6 Paperbound $1.25

HEAR ME TALKIN' TO YA: THE STORY OF JAZZ AS TOLD BY THE MEN WHO MADE IT, Nat Shapiro and Nat Hentoff. Louis Armstrong, Fats Waller, Jo Jones, Clarence Williams, Billy Holiday, Duke Ellington, Jelly Roll Morton and dozens of other jazz greats tell how it was in Chicago's South Side, New Orleans, depression Harlem and the modern West Coast as jazz was born and grew. xvi + 429pp.
21726-4 Paperbound $2.50

FABLES OF AESOP, translated by Sir Roger L'Estrange. A reproduction of the very rare 1931 Paris edition; a selection of the most interesting fables, together with 50 imaginative drawings by Alexander Calder. v + 128pp. 6½x9¼.
21780-9 Paperbound $1.50

AGAINST THE GRAIN (A REBOURS), Joris K. Huysmans. Filled with weird images, evidences of a bizarre imagination, exotic experiments with hallucinatory drugs, rich tastes and smells and the diversions of its sybarite hero Duc Jean des Esseintes, this classic novel pushed 19th-century literary decadence to its limits. Full unabridged edition. Do not confuse this with abridged editions generally sold. Introduction by Havelock Ellis. xlix + 206pp. 22190-3 Paperbound $2.00

VARIORUM SHAKESPEARE: HAMLET. Edited by Horace H. Furness; a landmark of American scholarship. Exhaustive footnotes and appendices treat all doubtful words and phrases, as well as suggested critical emendations throughout the play's history. First volume contains editor's own text, collated with all Quartos and Folios. Second volume contains full first Quarto, translations of Shakespeare's sources (Belleforest, and Saxo Grammaticus), Der Bestrafte Brudermord, and many essays on critical and historical points of interest by major authorities of past and present. Includes details of staging and costuming over the years. By far the best edition available for serious students of Shakespeare. Total of xx + 905pp. 21004-9, 21005-7, 2 volumes, Paperbound $7.00

A LIFE OF WILLIAM SHAKESPEARE, Sir Sidney Lee. This is the standard life of Shakespeare, summarizing everything known about Shakespeare and his plays. Incredibly rich in material, broad in coverage, clear and judicious, it has served thousands as the best introduction to Shakespeare. 1931 edition. 9 plates. xxix + 792pp. (USO) 21967-4 Paperbound $3.75

MASTERS OF THE DRAMA, John Gassner. Most comprehensive history of the drama in print, covering every tradition from Greeks to modern Europe and America, including India, Far East, etc. Covers more than 800 dramatists, 2000 plays, with biographical material, plot summaries, theatre history, criticism, etc. "Best of its kind in English," New Republic. 77 illustrations. xxii + 890pp. 20100-7 Clothbound $8.50

THE EVOLUTION OF THE ENGLISH LANGUAGE, George McKnight. The growth of English, from the 14th century to the present. Unusual, non-technical account presents basic information in very interesting form: sound shifts, change in grammar and syntax, vocabulary growth, similar topics. Abundantly illustrated with quotations. Formerly Modern English in the Making. xii + 590pp. 21932-1 Paperbound $3.50

AN ETYMOLOGICAL DICTIONARY OF MODERN ENGLISH, Ernest Weekley. Fullest, richest work of its sort, by foremost British lexicographer. Detailed word histories, including many colloquial and archaic words; extensive quotations. Do not confuse this with the Concise Etymological Dictionary, which is much abridged. Total of xxvii + 830pp. 6½ x 9¼. 21873-2, 21874-0 Two volumes, Paperbound $6.00

FLATLAND: A ROMANCE OF MANY DIMENSIONS, E. A. Abbott. Classic of science-fiction explores ramifications of life in a two-dimensional world, and what happens when a three-dimensional being intrudes. Amusing reading, but also useful as introduction to thought about hyperspace. Introduction by Banesh Hoffmann. 16 illustrations. xx + 103pp. 20001-9 Paperbound $1.00

POEMS OF ANNE BRADSTREET, edited with an introduction by Robert Hutchinson. A new selection of poems by America's first poet and perhaps the first significant woman poet in the English language. 48 poems display her development in works of considerable variety—love poems, domestic poems, religious meditations, formal elegies, "quaternions," etc. Notes, bibliography. viii + 222pp.

22160-1 Paperbound $2.50

THREE GOTHIC NOVELS: THE CASTLE OF OTRANTO BY HORACE WALPOLE; VATHEK BY WILLIAM BECKFORD; THE VAMPYRE BY JOHN POLIDORI, WITH FRAGMENT OF A NOVEL BY LORD BYRON, edited by E. F. Bleiler. The first Gothic novel, by Walpole; the finest Oriental tale in English, by Beckford; powerful Romantic supernatural story in versions by Polidori and Byron. All extremely important in history of literature; all still exciting, packed with supernatural thrills, ghosts, haunted castles, magic, etc. xl + 291pp.

21232-7 Paperbound $2.50

THE BEST TALES OF HOFFMANN, E. T. A. Hoffmann. 10 of Hoffmann's most important stories, in modern re-editings of standard translations: Nutcracker and the King of Mice, Signor Formica, Automata, The Sandman, Rath Krespel, The Golden Flowerpot, Master Martin the Cooper, The Mines of Falun, The King's Betrothed, A New Year's Eve Adventure. 7 illustrations by Hoffmann. Edited by E. F. Bleiler. xxxix + 419pp.

21793-0 Paperbound $3.00

GHOST AND HORROR STORIES OF AMBROSE BIERCE, Ambrose Bierce. 23 strikingly modern stories of the horrors latent in the human mind: The Eyes of the Panther, The Damned Thing, An Occurrence at Owl Creek Bridge, An Inhabitant of Carcosa, etc., plus the dream-essay, Visions of the Night. Edited by E. F. Bleiler. xxii + 199pp.

20767-6 Paperbound $1.50

BEST GHOST STORIES OF J. S. LEFANU, J. Sheridan LeFanu. Finest stories by Victorian master often considered greatest supernatural writer of all. Carmilla, Green Tea, The Haunted Baronet, The Familiar, and 12 others. Most never before available in the U. S. A. Edited by E. F. Bleiler. 8 illustrations from Victorian publications. xvii + 467pp.

20415-4 Paperbound $3.00

MATHEMATICAL FOUNDATIONS OF INFORMATION THEORY, A. I. Khinchin. Comprehensive introduction to work of Shannon, McMillan, Feinstein and Khinchin, placing these investigations on a rigorous mathematical basis. Covers entropy concept in probability theory, uniqueness theorem, Shannon's inequality, ergodic sources, the E property, martingale concept, noise, Feinstein's fundamental lemma, Shanon's first and second theorems. Translated by R. A. Silverman and M. D. Friedman. iii + 120pp.

60434-9 Paperbound $1.75

SEVEN SCIENCE FICTION NOVELS, H. G. Wells. The standard collection of the great novels. Complete, unabridged. *First Men in the Moon, Island of Dr. Moreau, War of the Worlds, Food of the Gods, Invisible Man, Time Machine, In the Days of the Comet.* Not only science fiction fans, but every educated person owes it to himself to read these novels. 1015pp. (USO) 20264-X Clothbound $5.00

LAST AND FIRST MEN AND STAR MAKER, TWO SCIENCE FICTION NOVELS, Olaf Stapledon. Greatest future histories in science fiction. In the first, human intelligence is the "hero," through strange paths of evolution, interplanetary invasions, incredible technologies, near extinctions and reemergences. Star Maker describes the quest of a band of star rovers for intelligence itself, through time and space: weird inhuman civilizations, crustacean minds, symbiotic worlds, etc. Complete, unabridged. v + 438pp. (USO) 21962-3 Paperbound $2.50

THREE PROPHETIC NOVELS, H. G. WELLS. Stages of a consistently planned future for mankind. *When the Sleeper Wakes,* and *A Story of the Days to Come,* anticipate *Brave New World* and *1984,* in the 21st Century; *The Time Machine,* only complete version in print, shows farther future and the end of mankind. All show Wells's greatest gifts as storyteller and novelist. Edited by E. F. Bleiler. x + 335pp. (USO) 20605-X Paperbound $2.50

THE DEVIL'S DICTIONARY, Ambrose Bierce. America's own Oscar Wilde— Ambrose Bierce—offers his barbed iconoclastic wisdom in over 1,000 definitions hailed by H. L. Mencken as "some of the most gorgeous witticisms in the English language." 145pp. 20487-1 Paperbound $1.25

MAX AND MORITZ, Wilhelm Busch. Great children's classic, father of comic strip, of two bad boys, Max and Moritz. Also Ker and Plunk (Plisch und Plumm), Cat and Mouse, Deceitful Henry, Ice-Peter, The Boy and the Pipe, and five other pieces. Original German, with English translation. Edited by H. Arthur Klein; translations by various hands and H. Arthur Klein. vi + 216pp.
20181-3 Paperbound $2.00

PIGS IS PIGS AND OTHER FAVORITES, Ellis Parker Butler. The title story is one of the best humor short stories, as Mike Flannery obfuscates biology and English. Also included, That Pup of Murchison's, The Great American Pie Company, and Perkins of Portland. 14 illustrations. v + 109pp. 21532-6 Paperbound $1.25

THE PETERKIN PAPERS, Lucretia P. Hale. It takes genius to be as stupidly mad as the Peterkins, as they decide to become wise, celebrate the "Fourth," keep a cow, and otherwise strain the resources of the Lady from Philadelphia. Basic book of American humor. 153 illustrations. 219pp. 20794-3 Paperbound $1.50

PERRAULT'S FAIRY TALES, translated by A. E. Johnson and S. R. Littlewood, with 34 full-page illustrations by Gustave Doré. All the original Perrault stories— Cinderella, Sleeping Beauty, Bluebeard, Little Red Riding Hood, Puss in Boots, Tom Thumb, etc.—with their witty verse morals and the magnificent illustrations of Doré. One of the five or six great books of European fairy tales. viii + 117pp. 8⅛ x 11. 22311-6 Paperbound $2.00

OLD HUNGARIAN FAIRY TALES, Baroness Orczy. Favorites translated and adapted by author of the *Scarlet Pimpernel.* Eight fairy tales include "The Suitors of Princess Fire-Fly," "The Twin Hunchbacks," "Mr. Cuttlefish's Love Story," and "The Enchanted Cat." This little volume of magic and adventure will captivate children as it has for generations. 90 drawings by Montagu Barstow. 96pp.
22293-4 Paperbound $1.95

THE RED FAIRY BOOK, Andrew Lang. Lang's color fairy books have long been children's favorites. This volume includes Rapunzel, Jack and the Bean-stalk and 35 other stories, familiar and unfamiliar. 4 plates, 93 illustrations x + 367pp.
21673-X Paperbound $2.50

THE BLUE FAIRY BOOK, Andrew Lang. Lang's tales come from all countries and all times. Here are 37 tales from Grimm, the Arabian Nights, Greek Mythology, and other fascinating sources. 8 plates, 130 illustrations. xi + 390pp.
21437-0 Paperbound $2.50

HOUSEHOLD STORIES BY THE BROTHERS GRIMM. Classic English-language edition of the well-known tales — Rumpelstiltskin, Snow White, Hansel and Gretel, The Twelve Brothers, Faithful John, Rapunzel, Tom Thumb (52 stories in all). Translated into simple, straightforward English by Lucy Crane. Ornamented with head-pieces, vignettes, elaborate decorative initials and a dozen full-page illustrations by Walter Crane. x + 269pp.
21080-4 Paperbound $2.00

THE MERRY ADVENTURES OF ROBIN HOOD, Howard Pyle. The finest modern versions of the traditional ballads and tales about the great English outlaw. Howard Pyle's complete prose version, with every word, every illustration of the first edition. Do not confuse this facsimile of the original (1883) with modern editions that change text or illustrations. 23 plates plus many page decorations. xxii + 296pp.
22043-5 Paperbound $2.50

THE STORY OF KING ARTHUR AND HIS KNIGHTS, Howard Pyle. The finest children's version of the life of King Arthur; brilliantly retold by Pyle, with 48 of his most imaginative illustrations. xviii + 313pp. 6⅛ x 9¼.
21445-1 Paperbound $2.50

THE WONDERFUL WIZARD OF OZ, L. Frank Baum. America's finest children's book in facsimile of first edition with all Denslow illustrations in full color. The edition a child should have. Introduction by Martin Gardner. 23 color plates, scores of drawings. iv + 267pp.
20691-2 Paperbound $2.50

THE MARVELOUS LAND OF OZ, L. Frank Baum. The second Oz book, every bit as imaginative as the Wizard. The hero is a boy named Tip, but the Scarecrow and the Tin Woodman are back, as is the Oz magic. 16 color plates, 120 drawings by John R. Neill. 287pp.
20692-0 Paperbound $2.50

THE MAGICAL MONARCH OF MO, L. Frank Baum. Remarkable adventures in a land even stranger than Oz. The best of Baum's books not in the Oz series. 15 color plates and dozens of drawings by Frank Verbeck. xviii + 237pp.
21892-9 Paperbound $2.25

THE BAD CHILD'S BOOK OF BEASTS, MORE BEASTS FOR WORSE CHILDREN, A MORAL ALPHABET, Hilaire Belloc. Three complete humor classics in one volume. Be kind to the frog, and do not call him names . . . and 28 other whimsical animals. Familiar favorites and some not so well known. Illustrated by Basil Blackwell. 156pp.
(USO) 20749-8 Paperbound $1.50

EAST O' THE SUN AND WEST O' THE MOON, George W. Dasent. Considered the best of all translations of these Norwegian folk tales, this collection has been enjoyed by generations of children (and folklorists too). Includes True and Untrue, Why the Sea is Salt, East O' the Sun and West O' the Moon, Why the Bear is Stumpy-Tailed, Boots and the Troll, The Cock and the Hen, Rich Peter the Pedlar, and 52 more. The only edition with all 59 tales. 77 illustrations by Erik Werenskiold and Theodor Kittelsen. xv + 418pp. 22521-6 Paperbound $3.50

GOOPS AND HOW TO BE THEM, Gelett Burgess. Classic of tongue-in-cheek humor, masquerading as etiquette book. 87 verses, twice as many cartoons, show mischievous Goops as they demonstrate to children virtues of table manners, neatness, courtesy, etc. Favorite for generations. viii + 88pp. 6½ x 9¼.
22233-0 Paperbound $1.25

ALICE'S ADVENTURES UNDER GROUND, Lewis Carroll. The first version, quite different from the final *Alice in Wonderland,* printed out by Carroll himself with his own illustrations. Complete facsimile of the "million dollar" manuscript Carroll gave to Alice Liddell in 1864. Introduction by Martin Gardner. viii + 96pp. Title and dedication pages in color. 21482-6 Paperbound $1.25

THE BROWNIES, THEIR BOOK, Palmer Cox. Small as mice, cunning as foxes, exuberant and full of mischief, the Brownies go to the zoo, toy shop, seashore, circus, etc., in 24 verse adventures and 266 illustrations. Long a favorite, since their first appearance in St. Nicholas Magazine. xi + 144pp. 6⅝ x 9¼.
21265-3 Paperbound $1.75

SONGS OF CHILDHOOD, Walter De La Mare. Published (under the pseudonym Walter Ramal) when De La Mare was only 29, this charming collection has long been a favorite children's book. A facsimile of the first edition in paper, the 47 poems capture the simplicity of the nursery rhyme and the ballad, including such lyrics as I Met Eve, Tartary, The Silver Penny. vii + 106pp. (USO) 21972-0 Paperbound $1.25

THE COMPLETE NONSENSE OF EDWARD LEAR, Edward Lear. The finest 19th-century humorist-cartoonist in full: all nonsense limericks, zany alphabets, Owl and Pussycat, songs, nonsense botany, and more than 500 illustrations by Lear himself. Edited by Holbrook Jackson. xxix + 287pp. (USO) 20167-8 Paperbound $2.00

BILLY WHISKERS: THE AUTOBIOGRAPHY OF A GOAT, Frances Trego Montgomery. A favorite of children since the early 20th century, here are the escapades of that rambunctious, irresistible and mischievous goat—Billy Whiskers. Much in the spirit of *Peck's Bad Boy,* this is a book that children never tire of reading or hearing. All the original familiar illustrations by W. H. Fry are included: 6 color plates, 18 black and white drawings. 159pp. 22345-0 Paperbound $2.00

MOTHER GOOSE MELODIES. Faithful republication of the fabulously rare Munroe and Francis "copyright 1833" Boston edition—the most important Mother Goose collection, usually referred to as the "original." Familiar rhymes plus many rare ones, with wonderful old woodcut illustrations. Edited by E. F. Bleiler. 128pp. 4½ x 6⅜. 22577-1 Paperbound $1.00

Two Little Savages; Being the Adventures of Two Boys Who Lived as Indians and What They Learned, Ernest Thompson Seton. Great classic of nature and boyhood provides a vast range of woodlore in most palatable form, a genuinely entertaining story. Two farm boys build a teepee in woods and live in it for a month, working out Indian solutions to living problems, star lore, birds and animals, plants, etc. 293 illustrations. vii + 286pp.

20985-7 Paperbound $2.50

Peter Piper's Practical Principles of Plain & Perfect Pronunciation. Alliterative jingles and tongue-twisters of surprising charm, that made their first appearance in America about 1830. Republished in full with the spirited woodcut illustrations from this earliest American edition. 32pp. 4½ x 6⅜.

22560-7 Paperbound $1.00

Science Experiments and Amusements for Children, Charles Vivian. 73 easy experiments, requiring only materials found at home or easily available, such as candles, coins, steel wool, etc.; illustrate basic phenomena like vacuum, simple chemical reaction, etc. All safe. Modern, well-planned. Formerly *Science Games for Children*. 102 photos, numerous drawings. 96pp. 6⅛ x 9¼.

21856-2 Paperbound $1.25

An Introduction to Chess Moves and Tactics Simply Explained, Leonard Barden. Informal intermediate introduction, quite strong in explaining reasons for moves. Covers basic material, tactics, important openings, traps, positional play in middle game, end game. Attempts to isolate patterns and recurrent configurations. Formerly *Chess*. 58 figures. 102pp. (USO) 21210-6 Paperbound $1.25

Lasker's Manual of Chess, Dr. Emanuel Lasker. Lasker was not only one of the five great World Champions, he was also one of the ablest expositors, theorists, and analysts. In many ways, his Manual, permeated with his philosophy of battle, filled with keen insights, is one of the greatest works ever written on chess. Filled with analyzed games by the great players. A single-volume library that will profit almost any chess player, beginner or master. 308 diagrams. xli x 349pp.

20640-8 Paperbound $2.75

The Master Book of Mathematical Recreations, Fred Schuh. In opinion of many the finest work ever prepared on mathematical puzzles, stunts, recreations; exhaustively thorough explanations of mathematics involved, analysis of effects, citation of puzzles and games. Mathematics involved is elementary. Translated by F. Göbel. 194 figures. xxiv + 430pp.

22134-2 Paperbound $3.00

Mathematics, Magic and Mystery, Martin Gardner. Puzzle editor for Scientific American explains mathematics behind various mystifying tricks: card tricks, stage "mind reading," coin and match tricks, counting out games, geometric dissections, etc. Probability sets, theory of numbers clearly explained. Also provides more than 400 tricks, guaranteed to work, that you can do. 135 illustrations. xii + 176pp.

20335-2 Paperbound $1.50